catching
readers

THE RESEARCH-INFORMED CLASSROOM SERIES

Consider daily life for a child struggling with reading. Imagine what it is like to go through school day after day feeling that you are bad at the one thing that school seems to value most. Imagine struggling with everything from independent reading to reading directions on a math worksheet. Imagine what that feels like. . . .

While there are all sorts of pressures to improve instruction for struggling readers—to raise test scores, to make adequate yearly progress (AYP), and so on—the most compelling reason is to help as many children as possible avoid that feeling. We want to enable children to go through elementary school feeling, and being, successful.

Barbara Taylor brings decades of research and development to the question of how to help struggling readers become successful. *Catching Readers, Grade K*, which is part of the Early Intervention in Reading series, brings the resulting insights to you, in the form of concrete and specific practices that have been shown to help children who struggle improve their reading. These books could not come at a more important time, as response to intervention (RTI) leads schools to invest more than ever in small-group reading instruction. The multifaceted and responsive teaching at the heart of the approach Taylor describes is a welcome contrast to the myopic, scripted programs marketed so heavily under the banner of RTI.

These books exemplify the ideals of the Research-Informed Classroom series— bringing rigorous classroom-based research to bear on persistent challenges of classroom practice. This series aims to bridge the gap between research and practice by focusing on the most practical, classroom-relevant research and communicating practices based on that research in a way that makes them accessible, appealing, and actionable. The series is founded on the belief that students and teachers are researchers' clients, and serving them should be the highest priority.

As with so much of the best educational research and development, Taylor has collaborated extensively with teachers close to home and throughout the United States. Indeed, one might say we've gone full circle, from Teacher-Informed Research to Research-Informed Teaching. So thank you, teachers, and thank you, Barbara, for this important contribution to reading success for all children.

—*Nell K. Duke*

MICHIGAN STATE UNIVERSITY

catching
readers

grade K

DAY-BY-DAY SMALL-GROUP READING INTERVENTIONS

Barbara M. Taylor

HEINEMANN
Portsmouth, NH

Heinemann
361 Hanover Street
Portsmouth, NH 03801–3912
www.heinemann.com

Offices and agents throughout the world

The author and publisher wish to thank those who have generously given permission to reprint borrowed material in this book and/or on the DVD:

Book cover from *Just Grandpa and Me* by Mercer Mayer. Copyright © 1983 by Random House Children's Books. Published by Random House Children's Books, a division of Random House, Inc. Reprinted by permission of the publisher.

Book cover and excerpts from *Mr. Gumpy's Outing* by John Burningham. Copyright © 1970 by John Burningham. Published by Henry Holt and Company, LLC. Reprinted by permission of the publisher.

Library of Congress Cataloging-in-Publication Data
Taylor, Barbara M.
   Catching readers, grade K : day-by-day small-group reading interventions / Barbara M. Taylor.
      p. cm.—(The early intervention in reading series) (The research-informed classroom series)
   Includes bibliographical references.
   ISBN-13: 978-0-325-02887-3
   ISBN-10: 0-325-02887-7
   1. Reading (Kindergarten). 2. Reading—Remedial teaching.
3. Individualized instruction. I. Title.
   LB1181.2.T39 2011
   372.4—dc22   2010054501

Editor: Margaret LaRaia
Production editor: Patricia Adams
Video editor: Sherry Day
Video producer: Bob Schuster, Real Productions
Cover design: Lisa Fowler
Typesetter: Eric Rosenbloom, Kirby Mountain Composition
Manufacturing: Steve Bernier

Printed in the United States of America on acid-free paper

15 14 13 12 11   ML   1 2 3 4 5

This book is dedicated to the many kindergarten teachers who work tirelessly to provide motivating instruction that meets their students' needs, challenges them all, and is instrumental to their success in reading.

Contents

1   What Does Effective Reading Instruction for Kindergartners Look Like?   1

2   Meet the Teachers
The Differentiated Lessons and Teacher Collaboration That Support EIR   17

On the DVD

See-It-in-Action Video Clips

Video 1 Talking About Text

Video 2 Acting Out a Story

Video 3 Hearing Beginning Sounds in Words

Video 4 Hearing Beginning and Ending Sounds in Words

Video 5 Blending Sounds into Words

Video 6 Learning Letter-Sound Correspondences

Video 7 Interactive Sentence Writing

Video 8 Tracking Print

Downloadable Classroom Reproducibles

More than 100 pages of full-size forms and teaching resources.

Teaching Resources on the DVD

Chapter 5

Chapter 6

Chapter 7

ADDITIONAL RESOURCES

Foreword

I began my teaching career as a first-grade teacher in Key West, Florida, in 1965. Much has changed since then in the world and in the world of school. But reading Barbara Taylor's books made me realize how much is still the same. My class of thirty-five children contained nine children—two girls and seven boys—who were (in the lingo of the day) "not ready." In those days, basal reading series for first grade had a readiness book that I was very grateful to find. I grouped these nine students together and we made our way through the workbook pages. The pages were mostly practice with letter names and auditory discrimination—the precursor of phonemic awareness. Six weeks into the school year, we finished the readiness book and I administered the Metropolitan Readiness Test to my students. For three days, I tried to keep them focused on the correct lines and asked them to underline the letter *b*, put an *x* on the picture that began like *paint*, and circle the picture of the object that rhymed with *cat*. I took all these booklets home and spent a miserable weekend grading them. As I made my way through the test booklets, I adopted a "benefit of the doubt" scoring system. "Two red marks on this line, none on the next. If the second mark is on the next line, it would be right. I'm counting it correct." In spite of my lenient scoring, scores for eight of the nine children indicated they were still "not ready." I spent a sleepless Sunday night wondering what I was to do with these children who were clearly not ready when I had used up all the readiness materials! Lacking any alternative, I started them in the first pre-primer and we plodded our way through the books. By the end of the year, only one of these students could read fluently at primer level.

If Barbara had written her books 45 years earlier (when she was probably in kindergarten), I think I could have transformed my "not ready" kids into fluent readers. Based on many years of research in real classrooms with real teachers and kids, Barbara has created a workable system for providing struggling readers in grades K–5 with the targeted intervention they need to become fluent readers. At the heart of Early Intervention in Reading (EIR) is the addition of a second reading lesson in a small-group setting. Unlike many interventions, struggling readers get this second reading lesson *in addition to* all the rich classroom instruction and *in* the classroom—not in some room down the hall. With details, specifics, and examples that only someone who has spent many hours in the classroom could know, Barbara guides you step-by-step as you organize for and provide effective EIR instruction. As you read through the book, your brain races with questions:

▶ "How do I fit an additional intervention group lesson into my daily schedule?"

▶ "What books work best for these lessons?"

▶ "How can I provide all the instruction struggling readers need in 20 minutes?"

▶ "What does the coaching for decoding and comprehension look like and sound like?"

▶ "How do I wean them off my coaching and move them toward independence?"

▶ "How do I provide worthwhile independent activities for the students I am not working with?"

Because Barbara has worked in so many classrooms coaching teachers who are implementing EIR, she can provide practical, classroom-tested answers to all your questions. She invites you into the classrooms of real teachers and you get to hear them describing how they organize and problem solve. In addition to the printed resource, you can go to the video clips on the DVD to "See It in Action." As you watch real teachers move through the three-day lesson sequence, you realize that, while it is complex, Barbara provides all the resources you need to make it work in your classrooms with your students who struggle.

Once you see how EIR works in your classroom, you will probably want to spread the word. Not to worry! Barbara is right there supporting you. In the final chapter, "Creating an EIR Community," she provides a detailed, month-by-month plan for organizing a group of colleagues to learn together how to better meet the needs of struggling readers.

So, if they ever invent a time machine that could transport me back to 1965, with the help of Barbara Taylor's books, I know I could teach all my "not ready" kids to read!

Patricia M. Cunningham
Wake Forest University

Acknowledgments

● ●

This book is the result of fifteen years of collaboration with many kindergarten teachers and colleagues across the United States. I want to thank them all for their invaluable contributions to this book.

Inspired by Reading Recovery, I developed the Early Intervention in Reading (EIR) process in the late 1980s to help first-grade teachers help their at-risk readers succeed in reading through daily, small-group, reading intervention lessons. I have refined the EIR process over the years by visiting many classrooms and learning from many teachers and their students. Without this opportunity, I would not have been able to modify and improve the EIR teaching strategies and professional learning practices described in this book.

I also want to thank the hundreds of kindergarten teachers I have visited and learned from over the past ten years through my work on effective reading instruction and schoolwide reading improvement. I especially want to thank the exemplary teachers who have contributed so much to the book by sharing their thoughts and lessons related to effective reading instruction.

I owe a special thanks and a debt of gratitude to my colleague, Ceil Critchely, a master teacher who has been instrumental in helping teachers succeed with EIR through the phenomenal professional learning support she has provided to them over the past twelve years. I know that without Ceil's expert guidance, teachers would not have been as successful as they have been in helping their at-risk readers learn to read well in first grade.

I also want to thank my academic colleagues for their support and feedback. In particular, I want to recognize my good friends, Kathy Au and Taffy Raphael, who have gently nudged me over the years to publish my work on EIR in a form readily accessible to teachers.

I want to thank the many people at Heinemann who have made this book possible. Thanks to Patty Adams, my production editor, for her top-notch work on a complex project within a challenging time frame. Whenever I called with questions or concerns, she responded cheerfully and promptly. Many others at Heinemann have also contributed to this book and I thank them for their efforts.

It is my sincere hope that kindergarten teachers will find this book useful as they strive to teach students who come to them a little behind in the fall to be confident, successful, readers by the end of the school year. Thanks to all kindergarten teachers reading this book for the important work you do for our children!

Barbara M. Taylor
University of Minnesota

Introduction

W̲e are a culture of quick fixes. We promise mastery in ten easy lessons, instant success, overnight sensations. Go to a bookstore and whether you stand and gaze at the brightly colored covers in the business, health, or education section, the answer to our every need is couched in words like *speedy*, *easy*, and *seven easy steps*.

In such a culture, a lot of alarm bells go off when a teacher faces a five-year-old child in kindergarten who is behind in emergent reading abilities. *Catching Readers, Grade K,* is one book in a series of five, dedicated to giving the regular classroom teacher what's needed to reach and teach that five-year-old with a concrete plan rather than a frantic pull-out program or a misguided label. Each book in the series offers teacher-friendly, research-proven background and lessons for young readers who need an extra boost.

The intervention model brings reading success to children in a five-day lesson cycle, which I know sounds as though I'm playing into the same glib promises of swift solutions. I state it here as a way to express that it is a five-day format used across a school year with deep roots—more than fifteen years of classroom testing. I emphasize the "five-day" repetition of the lessons to make it clear that we don't have to choose to run around in circles looking for some new complicated program for reaching at-risk readers. We know what to do. When we're true to children's developmental levels, know which books to put in their hands, and provide effective instruction, a lot of good things fall into place. The key is to focus on the children and the practices we know help them to read at each grade level.

In fact, the intervention model I offer stands in opposition to approaches and programs that think the answer to helping K–5 below-grade-level readers achieve is to provide remediation. Above-grade-level, on-grade-level, and below-grade-level readers all need the same thing: sound teaching techniques and developmentally appropriate practices that meet their needs and provide intellectual challenge to all.

Here's an overview of how the interventions are unique and yet similar for each grade level, so you can see the developmentally based, purposeful overlap in the series. The intervention gives teachers, staff developers, principals, and reading coaches a predictable model so that schoolwide coherence is easier to attain. All grade-level models stress word-recognition proficiency, high-level comprehension, vocabulary development, and strategic reading. Unique components of the various grade-specific models are described below:

Kindergarten

The daily 10-minute supplemental lessons for kindergarten focus on developing all children's oral language, phonemic awareness, and emergent literacy abilities through literature-based activities. The goal is for all students to leave kindergarten with the skills they need to learn to read in first grade. The more capable children, as they respond to the various activities in EIR lessons, serve as models for the children who are less skilled in oral language and emergent literacy abilities. Less-skilled children who need more support return to some of the story discussion questions and phonemic awareness/emergent literacy activities for an additional 10 minutes a day.

First Grade

First-grade children who start the school year with lower-than-average phonemic awareness abilities and letter-sound knowledge will benefit from EIR lessons. The teacher focuses on accelerating students' literacy learning by deliberately coaching them to use strategies to decode words as they read, to actively engage in word work, and to think at a higher level about the meaning of the texts they are reading.

Second Grade

Second-grade readers who can't read a book at a first-grade level at the start of second grade will benefit from the basic EIR routine. The intervention begins with first-grade books and routines of the grade 1 EIR model and then moves into second-grade books a few months later. There is also an accelerated grade 2 routine designed for students who come to second grade as independent readers but who will need additional support to be reading on grade level by the end of the school year.

Third Grade

The grade 3 EIR routine is for children who are reading below grade level when they enter third grade. In the grade 3 EIR model, the focus is on refining students' decoding of multisyllabic words, improving their fluency, developing their vocabulary, and enhancing their comprehension of narrative and informational texts. Ideally, the grade 3 EIR model is done within the context of a cross-age tutoring program in which the third-grade students read to and also tutor first-grade EIR students. The third graders are working on their reading for more than "catching up because they are behind." They look forward to and enjoy working with their younger student who needs additional support in reading.

Fourth/Fifth Grade

The EIR routine for fourth and fifth grade is for children who are reading below grade level at the beginning of the school year. Although students receive support in attacking multisyllabic words and developing reading fluency, the grade 4/5 model focuses on improving students' comprehension of informational text through the use of comprehension strategies, discussion of vocabulary, and engagement in high-level talk and writing about texts. Ideally, the grade 4/5 EIR model is done within the context of a motivating cross-age tutoring program in which fourth and fifth graders read to and also tutor second or third graders.

Getting Good at It: Different Ways to Use This Book

This book—and by extension all the books in this series—is designed to be used by the individual teacher, a pair or group of teachers, or as part of a schoolwide professional development plan. Here are components that support collaborative learning:

Video Clips for Individual Viewing

As you read about the recurring cycle of EIR routines, I encourage you to watch the video clips that illustrate what is being covered in the text. Many teachers have told me that seeing the EIR routines being applied in the classroom makes it easy to start teaching the EIR lessons. See this icon throughout the book for easy access to the video clips and teaching resources on the DVD.

Guidance for Monthly Sessions with Colleagues

In the last chapter, "Creating an EIR Community," I share a model for a professional learning community (PLC) that works. Over my many years of working with teachers on effective reading instruction generally, and EIR lessons specifically, I have learned from teachers' comments that the collaborative nature of learning new instructional techniques with colleagues leads to excellent understanding, reflection, and success.

Website Support

For additional support, go to www.Heinemann.com and search by Taylor or *Catching Readers.* Also visit www.earlyinterventioninreading.com to learn more about the availability of additional support from an EIR expert.

We can help so many children become successful readers when we offer excellent reading instruction and provide effective interventions to those students who require additional reading support within their classroom setting. I am excited to have the opportunity to offer my *Catching Readers* series of books to you. Thank you for the important work you do for our children!

catching
readers

grade K

What Does Effective Reading Instruction for Kindergartners Look Like?

K indergarten is an important year in children's developing literacy. Kindergarten teachers meet a dramatic range of students in the fall, from the child who knows only a few letters of the alphabet to the child who walks in on the first day already a reader. It takes years for kindergarten teachers to hone their expertise to meet the needs of their emergent readers, teaching them beginning reading skills and getting them ready to become independent readers in first grade (or in some cases teaching them to read before they enter first grade). This book and the companion video clips and teacher resources on the DVD will help teachers arrive at this level of effectiveness sooner.

My career as a researcher and teacher educator has been dedicated to studying and describing components of effective literacy instruction so that teachers can become more intentional in their teaching and more confident in their interactions with children during all the aspects of reading instruction. Through this book, my goal is for you to be able to teach efficient, effective whole-group emergent reading lessons as well as follow-up small-group reading lessons for young children who struggle with reading. I will also show you how emergent reading lessons and intervention work to connect and inform all the rich literacy practices that occur within a balanced literacy framework.

How the Early Intervention in Reading Model Sits Within Effective Reading Instruction

The emergent literacy lessons featured in this book are based on EIR®, which is a set of teaching practices I developed that incorporates the characteristics of effective reading instruction (see page 3). EIR has been used in schools for almost twenty years and can easily become the conduit for implementing response to intervention (RTI) or differentiated instruction. Early Intervention in Reading provides:

▶ kindergartners who are struggling with emergent reading activities an additional daily opportunity to interact with text in a structured, consistent, and comfortable small-group setting

▶ kindergarten teachers with a repetitive, clear structure that can help them provide a sound scope and sequence of emergent literacy lessons, as well as follow-up support for children who need more coaching in order to catch up or keep up with grade-level expectations

▶ teachers and schools an intervention model that isn't stigmatizing for children because it uses authentic literature and practices, and takes place within the regular classroom—and usually by the classroom teacher

I developed this model because I don't believe kindergartners should be pulled out of the classroom for extra help. Rather, all teachers need to work together so that all children get a good start in reading. Supplemental instruction for those who are struggling can't be something only specialized reading teachers know about.

Through structured 10- or 15-minute whole-class lessons and 10-minute follow-up lessons, all students receive effective emergent reading instruction and struggling readers receive an extra dose of it. When you as their regular classroom teacher adapt lessons and support based on each student's needs, progress is accelerated. And, knowing that this is a model that has decades of research and practice behind it, you are more likely to commit to using it consistently; seeing your students make striking gains is highly motivating. We'll look at the weekly lesson activities in detail later in the book, but first, here's a glimpse of how these lessons extend and amplify the effective reading instruction you provide to all your students.

How EIR Meets the Requirements of Effective Reading Instruction

	Effective Reading Instruction	EIR Lessons
What You Teach (Content)	Explicit phonemic awareness	Listening for sounds in words, blending sounds to make words, working with sound boxes, and writing letters representing sounds into words in sentences
	Explicit systematic phonics	Learning and reviewing letter names and practice letter-sound recognition, working with sound boxes, writing letters representing sounds into words in sentences, and working with word families
	Concepts of print	Modeling how to track, tracking while "reading" simple texts many times over
	Text-based vocabulary and concepts	Discussing word meanings and concepts at the point they are encountered
	Comprehension, in the context of high-level talk about text	Regularly and actively talking about texts
	Comprehension strategies	Summarizing stories and informational text
How You Teach (Pedagogy)	Apply taught skills and strategies to text	Applying taught skills and strategies to text
	Differentiate instruction	Supporting individual students based on need
	Balance teaching directly and providing support	Coaching students as they use skills and strategies while working on phonemic awareness, decoding, writing, and reading and discussing stories
	Teach with a clear purpose and good timing	Stating the purpose of each 10- or 15-minute lesson clearly and routinely, then presenting it efficiently
	Actively engage students	Listening, writing, talking, and sharing with a partner, and working with words
	Engage students in challenging, motivating learning activities	Listening to engaging, well-written stories that motivate them to think
	Develop independent learners	Keeping high expectations, releasing responsibility to students as they work together on their own
	Motive	Offering praise and helpful feedback as you demonstrate enthusiasm for learning
Professional Learning	Collaborative learning with a focus on practice	In monthly learning meetings, discuss EIR strategies, successes, and challenges with your colleagues

Which Children Need the Intervention and What Is the End Goal

EIR lessons benefit all kindergartners and especially those who have relatively weak letter-name and letter-sound knowledge and phonemic awareness. These students are likely to struggle with reading in first grade. The strategies are effective within the context of many types of regular reading programs (e.g., basal, whole language, reading and writing workshop, systematic phonics). In Chapter 5, I describe assessments you can use to determine which students might benefit from EIR.

Does the Intervention Work?

Three research studies have shown that students who participated in EIR in kindergarten had higher phonemic awareness scores in the spring than comparable students who did not receive early intervention (see the research section of the DVD). Looking at twenty-four schools (Taylor 2001), I found that the 700 kindergarten students who participated in EIR lessons had a mean phonemic awareness score of 7 in May. My earlier research (Taylor 1991) showed that kindergartners who score 6 or higher on this test are likely to succeed in learning to read in grade 1.

A Brief Review of How Children Learn to Read

To most effectively help struggling readers learn how to read, you need to have a clear model of what children are learning to do. The following elements discussed tend to be the ones struggling beginning readers have the most trouble internalizing.

The Role of Phonemic Awareness

Phonemic awareness, or the ability to hear the sounds in words and to blend those sounds together, is one of the two best predictors of reading achievement by the end of first grade. Adams (1990), the National Reading Panel (2000), and Snow et al. (1998) have shown that children who come to first grade with low phonemic awareness are at considerable risk of failing to learn to read in first grade. (The other predictor is whether children know the names of letters. However, simply teaching children the letter names in kindergarten and first grade does *not* have a big impact on their May reading achievement.) Fortunately, kindergarten interventions, as well as interventions in early first grade, can make a big difference in accelerating children's phonemic awareness and hence impact their reading achievement.

Phonemic awareness is an auditory skill. Segmenting sounds, blending sounds, hearing alliteration, and recognizing rhymes are all measures of phonemic awareness. However, the two measures most predictive of end-of-first-grade reading achievement are the ability to segment phonemes (for example, separate the sounds in the word *cat* into /c/ /a/ /t/) and blend phonemes (combine the sounds /c/ /a/ /t/ into the word *cat*) (Adams 1990; NRP 2000; Snow et al. 1998).

Partial Decoding and Grasping the Alphabetic Principle

Children begin reading by partially decoding words and using context cues. They typically start using the first letter to sound out a word but cannot get all the way through a word. Beginning readers sometimes overrely on context to figure out words. The downward arrows in Figure 1–1 represent the "aha" moment when children finally understand the alphabetic principle, or how to sound out words. When they get to this point, they understand that within a printed word there are letters that represent phonemes (sounds) that have to be voiced separately and blended together to become a word. Adults often fail to realize just how challenging this understanding is for children to develop. But many children come to first grade not knowing what makes up a printed word and not knowing what the sounds are in a given word (this isn't too surprising; they have never needed to know about the separate sounds in words before).

Because the alphabetic principle seems a simple concept to us now, we adults think that if we explain it, children should catch on quickly. Most first graders (and some kindergartners) do grasp the alphabetic principle fairly quickly in the fall and their reading ability soars. Unfortunately, most children who need EIR lessons don't fully grasp the alphabetic principle until January or February of first grade, and once they do, their ability to decode improves slowly. Some children receiving EIR—about one-third—don't grasp the

Stages of Word Recognition Development

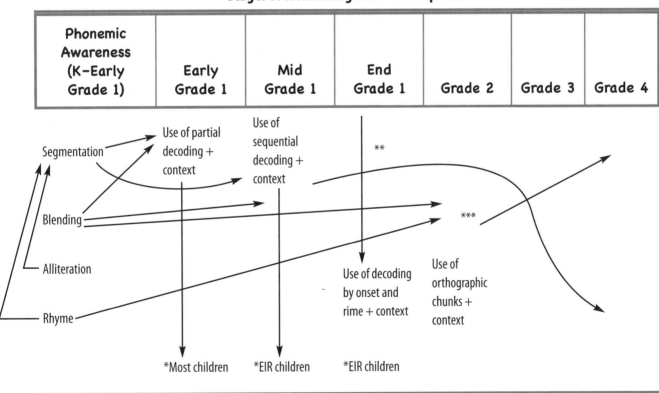

Figure 1–1 Stages of Word Recognition Development

alphabetic principle until April or May. Over the years I've come to accept this slower development. We need to be patient, believe in the children, and keep working with them. I am always impressed with the incredible patience demonstrated by the teachers I visit who are using these strategies with their struggling readers.

Learning How to Decode Letter by Letter and by Onset and Rime

EIR instruction emphasizes teaching children to use word-recognition strategies on their own. Sequential letter-by-letter decoding is only one of those strategies, but it is one that is very important to becoming an independent reader. When children come to the word *pig*, they need to be able to sound out each letter, /p/ /i/ /g/, and blend the sounds together into *pig*. Teachers begin to work on sequential letter-by-letter decoding with students in kindergarten, and first-grade teachers need to model and coach the strategy repeatedly.

Students can decode by onset and rime—the initial sound and the phonogram that completes the word: /f/ /ind/, *find*—when prompted to do so, and teachers begin to model this in kindergarten. However, students do not decode by onset and rime independently until they understand sequential letter-by-letter decoding. (See "A Brief Review of Research on the Learning-to-Read Process," Taylor 1998, on the DVD.)

As children start to "glue to the print" (pay attention to the sequence of letters), they rely much less on context to help them decode words. Reminding children to think about what would make sense in the story as they are sounding out words makes it easier for them to come up with the correct word.

By the end of first grade and early into second grade, decoding by onset and rime becomes children's preferred decoding strategy, because recognizing a chunk (e.g., phonogram) is quicker than sequential letter-by-letter decoding (Taylor 1998).

Developing Automaticity

The goal in teaching children to recognize words is that they eventually are able to do so automatically. By second grade and into third grade, children are reading most words on sight. This doesn't mean we have to drill them in this; while reading for meaning, children automatically recognize specific words because of repeated exposure to them.

In time children recognize most words automatically and no longer depend on context to help them. Of course, they will come across words that they have never seen before, but for the most part, by fourth grade, students typically read with context-free, automatic word recognition.

The Role of Comprehension and Vocabulary

Since the purpose of reading is to gain meaning from the text, it is important to stress both comprehension and vocabulary with emerging readers. Too often, especially with struggling readers, instruction emphasizes breaking the code and neglects reading for meaning. We need to keep in mind that decoding improves as comprehension improves and trust the interconnectedness of these two processes. Effective kindergarten teachers, as we see in the lessons of Choua Zhang, Stan Wolff, and Lena Jacobson in Chapter 2, emphasize reading for meaning and enjoyment. In EIR lessons, teachers also stress comprehension by including it every day in whole-group and small-group follow-up lessons.

The What and How of Good Kindergarten Teaching

EIR was developed with key elements of content (the what) and pedagogy (the how) as its foundation. Effective teachers are aware, day to day, of both content and pedagogy. Having a good grasp of the content and pedagogy of effective reading instruction will inform your practice and help you make day-to-day decisions about your reading lessons. In turn, these effective practices will help your students develop into motivated, competent readers.

In Chapter 2 you will meet three teachers—Choua Zhang, Stan Wolff, and Lena Jacobson—who demonstrate what effective teaching looks like in urban, suburban, and rural settings. You'll gain a sense of how these teachers connect EIR lessons to their overall reading instruction. These three teachers not only teach these specialized lessons but also provide effective reading instruction to all their students and see excellent growth in their students' reading abilities during each school year.

Content: Four Dimensions Young Children Need

Effective elementary school reading instruction has many dimensions, all of which develop the abilities students need to become competent readers. The main dimensions are:

- word-recognition development (including phonemic awareness and phonics)

- fluency development (once students are independent readers)

- vocabulary development

- comprehension development

Do these elements alone lead children to become successful, engaged readers? No, but these are the nonnegotiable aspects of teaching reading. Without them, all the other practices—from reading picture books aloud to independent reading—will not have a sufficient foundation.

Word-Recognition Development

Most students, especially those in kindergarten and first grade, benefit from systematic, explicit instruction in phonemic awareness and phonics (Adams 1990; National Reading Panel [NRP] 2000; Snow et al. 1998). Teaching students in kindergarten and in the fall of first grade to hear the sounds in words and blend these sounds into words are the most important aspects of phonemic awareness for learning to read. However, you do not need to overdo this instruction. Between fifteen and eighteen hours total in kindergarten is sufficient (NRP 2000).

A number of approaches to systematic phonics instruction are effective, including letter-by-letter decoding and decoding by onset and rime (Christensen and Bowey 2005; Juel and Minden-Cupp 2000: Mathes et al. 2005; NRP 2000). Coaching students to use word-recognition strategies as they read stories and informational texts is another important aspect of decoding instruction. For example, in the next chapter, teacher Stan Wolff talks to a small group of above-average readers about sounding out *dig* letter-by-letter as they read from a leveled text.

Fluency Development

Developing *fluency*, or reading at a good rate with appropriate phrasing, is important, because fluent reading supports comprehension. When students receive guidance or support during oral reading, the impact on students' reading abilities is significant (Kuhn and Stahl 2003). Procedures to build fluency include repeated reading and coached reading, as well as ample opportunities to read just-right books. Effective reading instruction weaves the practice of fluency into whole-group and small-group lessons and independent work. In kindergarten, teachers can help emergent readers focus on rereading predictable texts with good fluency, phrasing, and expression.

Vocabulary Development

Taking a variety of approaches toward developing students' vocabulary is critical (Baumann and Kame'enui 2004; Blachowicz and Fisher 2000; Graves 2007). The approaches include:

▶ teaching specific words through direct instruction

▶ providing word instruction prior to reading

▶ teaching strategies for determining word meanings

▶ exposing students to words in rich contexts through read-alouds and by encouraging them to read widely

▶ studying words that children will find useful in many contexts (Beck et al. 2002)

Three points are worth emphasizing. First, some words need to be introduced before reading so that students are not confused about a major aspect of a story. When Lena Jacobson introduces an informational text about penguins that need to be rescued from an oil spill, she talks about the meaning of *rescue* before they listen to the text. She models making a connection to the word by sharing a time someone rescued her when she was a child, then has students share with a partner a time they rescued someone or something or were themselves rescued.

Second, teachers sometimes provide insufficient vocabulary instruction *during* the reading of a story. Beck and colleagues (2002) stress the value of teaching many word meanings at the point they are encountered in the text. When Lena reads the first page of the book about penguins, she stops briefly to tell students what oil is and to have them share ideas about why oil might kill penguins.

Third, developing students' interest in words is also important. You can model this interest in word meanings and enthusiasm for authors' word choice in a variety of ways, and it's a boon to students' reading and writing. For example, after Lena has read *Hattie and the Fox* (Fox 1986) and they discuss the meaning of "Goodness gracious me," students have fun repeating this phrase expressively when they share something they are surprised about: "Goodness gracious me, I see [*a dinosaur in the yard*] [*a blue bunny across the street*]."

Comprehension Development

Skilled readers use strategies as they read to enhance their comprehension. Researchers have shown that instruction in comprehension strategies improves students' ability to understand what they read (Foorman et al. 2006; Guthrie et al. 2000; NRP 2000). Explicit lessons in the following strategies are most effective: summarizing; monitoring comprehension; using graphic and semantic organizers before, during, and after reading; using story structure; and generating and answering questions. Also, using a number of instructional strategies, like reciprocal teaching, in naturalistic contexts is important (Guthrie et al. 2004; Klingner et al. 2004; NRP 2000; Pressley 2006). The classroom examples in Chapter 2 include instruction in summarizing a story, summarizing information text, and asking and answering questions. After reading about animals taking care of their young, Choua Zhang asks questions that prompt her students to summarize the big ideas ("Mothers keep their babies clean; mothers watch their babies as they sleep").

Teaching students how to engage in high-level talk and writing about text is another vital aspect of comprehension instruction (Knapp 1995; McKeown et al. 2009; Saunders and Goldenberg 1999; Taylor et al. 2003; Van den Branden 2000). For example, after reading *The Little Red Hen* in an EIR whole-group lesson, Stan asks students what the author's message is. Students quickly offer ideas such as, "You should help other people. You should be nice and help out."

Reflecting on the author's message or big ideas in a text allow readers to understand the story at a deeper level than simply recalling story events. Kindergartners are often much more capable of high-level talk than teachers realize, and can make remarkable connections with and inferences and statements about a story's big ideas and the motivations of its characters.

Pedagogy: The Art of Teaching Demystified

With these content elements under our belt, let's turn to the *how* behind the *what*: the essential pedagogy behind EIR lessons and all effective teaching. We know good teaching when we see it, and yet it can be hard to capture all the nuances in the confines of a book. In short, it's all the routines and practices a teacher uses, as well as the ability to respond in the moment to students' needs and to connect to students so they feel motivated to learn. Techniques include clearly stating lesson purposes, impromptu coaching, and making decisions about timing (e.g., how long to spend on a particular aspect of a lesson) or what texts and tasks to use to engage students in purposeful learning activities. As you read the characteristics that follow, think about your kindergarten students and how you view yourself in relation to these aspects of effective teaching.

Affective dimensions and people skills are other important aspects of pedagogy in teaching reading. Research and our own experiences have a lot to tell us about the impact of teachers' management, expectations, and attitudes toward learning on children's achievement and motivation. As you read the list of effective classroom management characteristics and interaction practices, think about how you exemplify these aspects of effective teaching.

Brief, Daily Lessons on Essential Emergent Literacy Activities

The EIR model, like other successful early intervention models, is built on research (see Taylor 2001). Emerging readers who start out a little behind need to experience success quickly, and EIR is structured to make this happen. Each week, two or three books are read several times for different purposes. This predictable structure provides consistency for struggling readers and helps build their confidence. During a daily 10- or 15-minute whole-group lesson and 10-minute follow-up lesson for students who are struggling, students:

- Become actively engaged
- Systematically learn about systematic phonemic awareness and phonics
- Develop concepts of print
- Learn comprehension strategies and increase their vocabulary
- Read and talk about simple texts
- Write about what they read
- Have their progress regularly monitored

Active Engagement

Throughout the whole-group session, students actively participate in multiple activities with several books that address different elements essential to learning to read (see Figure 1–2). The follow-up session is considered to be acceleration, not remediation, so that struggling readers do learn the emergent literacy abilities needed to become independent readers before they fall way behind.

Elements of Effective Pedagogy

Effective teachers skillfully coordinate many pedagogical aspects of their reading lessons. They make sure that they:

▶ Strike a good balance between whole-group and small-group instruction, using the form that best meets lesson objectives (Chorzempa and Graham 2006)

▶ Consider the purposes and timing of their lessons relative to their students' varying instructional needs

▶ Balance direct teaching (telling, leading) with differentiated support (coaching, providing feedback) (Connor et al. 2004; Pressley et al. 2003; Taylor et al. 2003)

▶ Foster students' active involvement in literacy activities to enhance their learning and motivation (Guthrie et al. 2000)

▶ Use challenging, motivating activities whether students are working with you, on their own, or with other students (Pressley et al. 2003)

▶ Maintain a balance between teaching reading skills and strategies directly and giving students opportunities to apply these skills and strategies by reading, listening to, writing about, and discussing engaging texts (Pressley 2006)

▶ Differentiate instruction and choose instructional materials based on students' abilities and interests (Pressley et al. 2007)

▶ Offer culturally responsive instruction: build on students' cultural strengths during student interactions and use multicultural literature to celebrate students' cultural heritages and introduce students to new cultural perspectives (Au 2006)

▶ Assess students' engagement, understanding, and behavior throughout the day (Pressley et al. 2003)

▶ Systematically collect and share a variety of formal and informal student assessment data—diagnostic, formative (as kids work), and summative (check whether students understand)—and use this information to make instructional decisions to improve student performance (Lipson et al. 2004; Taylor et al. 2000)

Systematic Word Recognition Instruction

Your initial instructional focus is on developing phonemic awareness, teaching letter names and letter-sound recognition, and helping students write for sounds. You go on to emphasize tracking and sounding out words as students read simple texts. Some of your phonemic awareness and phonics instruction is provided through word work after students have read or listened to a story (see Figure 1–2; these activities are introduced in Chapter 3 and described in detail in Chapter 4).

Coaching in Word-Recognition Strategies

When children are reading simple texts at the end of the school year, you help them figure out words they don't instantly recognize by modeling, asking questions, and prompting. Typically, when a child is asked, "What do you do when you come to a word you don't know?" he answers, "Sound it out." That's one good strategy, but you want them to realize readers do other things when they come to words they don't recognize. As a coach, you need to prompt children to use a variety of word-recognition strategies, not overemphasize a single strategy, so they learn they have a repertoire of strategies to use to decode words. As Lena reads a leveled text about animal legs with a small group, she refers them to a chart of word-recognition strategies they can use, including looking at the picture, sounding it out, and looking for a chunk.

Coaching also helps children learn to monitor their word recognition—that is, correct on their own a word they've initially read incorrectly. Complimenting children for their attempts ("Good checking, how did you know to try that word again?") is an integral part of the instruction: both the praise and the question encourage children to be aware of the strategies they are using to make sense of the text. Students will begin to notice when words they say don't make sense in the context of the story or don't look like the word they are trying to read. Part of self-monitoring is learning to cross-check—to be sure that a

Guided Writing for Sounds

After listening to a story or informational book, you and the children together write a sentence about the story. After listening to *Jump, Frog, Jump* (Kalan 1981), students might help you write, "The frog jumped away." At first you model writing the sounds you hear in the words with students' help. Later, students write a group or individual sentence by themselves with your support. After listening to *Just Grandpa and Me* (Mayer 1985) in the spring, students might all write, "He went to the store." (Video 7 on the DVD shows a teacher coaching her students as they each write this sentence on a whiteboard.) By trying to turn the sounds they use to communicate an idea about the story into letters and words, children refine their phonemic awareness, develop their understanding of the alphabetic principle, and learn letter-sound correspondence.

Elkonin Sound Boxes

This activity develops phonemic awareness as well as letter-name knowledge, letter-sound knowledge, and the ability to decode sequentially letter-by-letter. Children listen for sounds in the words used in the stories they are reading and write the letters for these sounds in a string of boxes. For example, if a story is about a hen, you would ask students to listen for the sounds in the word *hen,* and, as they say the word, write *h* in the first box, *e* in the second, and *n* in the third.

Creating Word Families

After about three months, you and your students begin writing words that belong to the same family as a word used in a story (Cunningham 2009). For example, after reading "A caterpillar will become a moth or a butterfly, but first it needs to grow and change," you and your students might write *but* on whiteboards, then write *cut* and *nut*, and talk about how these words all have the *-ut* ending.

word not only looks like the word on the page but also makes sense in the story, and vice versa. Lena asks students reading the text about animal legs, "How do you know this word is *beetle,* not *bug*? They say that the word has *ee* "for long *e*" in it and is too long to be *bug*.

Concepts of Print

Even though many kindergartners will not be able to track print on their own, you should model this frequently during the year. As you read sentences from stories that you have put on the board or on a chart (or, in the spring, as students read short books and summaries), model tracking and reading from left to right and from one line of text to the next. Also, as the students and you write sentences interactively, focus on leaving spaces between words, writing from left to right, using punctuation, and so on. Students can practice tracking as they reread the sentence you've written together.

Comprehension and Vocabulary Instruction

To send the message that meaning is what reading is all about, discuss the meanings of potentially unfamiliar words you come across in texts. You should also ask questions about the stories students read, questions that expand their comprehension of the story, stretch their thinking, prompt them to relate the story to their lives, or involve them in summarizing. As students answer these questions, coach them to elaborate on their ideas. Since there is a lot to cover in the 10- or 15-minute lesson, you won't be able to give every child a chance to answer a question every day. However, during the week you're focusing on a story, you should be able to give all children a chance to answer one of your questions.

Small-Group Follow-Up Practice

Every day you'll meet for 10 minutes with the students who are struggling the most with literacy and review what you covered in the whole-group lesson. As these children practice the same emergent reading skills and answer the same comprehension questions with your support in a small group, they typically experience greater success.

Regular Monitoring of Progress

Regular monitoring of students' progress is a hallmark of effective teachers and schools (Lipson et al. 2004; Pressley et al. 2003; Taylor et al. 2000). Using a checklist of essential beginning reading skills, you'll assess your students' reading abilities frequently so you'll know when to fine-tune your instruction. You may need to provide more help or give them more responsibility in order to accelerate their reading growth. Children who know most of the letter names and sounds and can segment and blend the sounds in three- and four-phoneme words by the end of kindergarten are making good progress in learning to read (Taylor 2011b). (See Chapter 5 for more information on assessment.)

How the EIR Model Fits Within a Balanced Literacy Block

Let's look at how you might fit EIR lessons into a 110- to 120-minute daily block of reading instruction during a full day of kindergarten (or a 90-minute block during a half-day program).

A Sample Schedule

Choua Zhang has a 120-minute reading block. She spends about 25 minutes a day on a whole-group lesson from the school's core reading program and

Reading Block: Choua's Sample Schedule

9:00–9:25 Whole-Group Lesson

- Use a selection from a basal reader or trade book
- Target a comprehension skill or strategy
- Teach vocabulary at point of contact in the selection
- Pose and discuss answers to high-level questions
- Review learning activities for independent work time

9:30–10:30 Independent and Small-Group Work

Independent Work: While I work with small groups of students, the other students work independently or with a partner or small group on challenging and differentiated materials. (See Chapter 6 for a more in-depth discussion of independent work activities.) Students might:

- Work with me on words encountered in their guided reading group lesson
- Write and draw in a journal or on open-ended response sheets about what they have read
- Listen to a story on tape and talk with others about what they have read
- Write down new or interesting vocabulary and possible word meanings
- Read/reread books in their book baskets or book bags

Small Group 1 (9:30–9:45)

Using a story at students' reading level, I:

- Provide phonemic awareness and phonics instruction as needed
- Coach students in word-recognition strategies as they read the story
- Discuss vocabulary at point of contact in the story
- Provide follow-up instruction to the comprehension skill/strategy targeted in the whole-group lesson
- Pose and discuss answers to high-level questions about the story

Small Group 2 (9:50–10:05)

Follow same strategies as small-group 1.

Small Group 3 (10:10–10:25)

Follow same strategies as small-group 1.

10:30–10:45 EIR Whole-Group Lesson

Follow EIR strategies.

10:50–11:00 EIR Small-Group Follow-Up Work

Reinforce EIR strategies. (These students were also in small group 1, 2, or 3.)

15 minutes on an EIR whole-group lesson. She spends about an hour a day on three guided reading groups and 10 minutes on one EIR small-group follow-up lesson (the second dose of quality small-group instruction she gives her students who need more support). See the previous page for an example of her schedule.

In the next chapter, three teachers share how the content and pedagogy of effective reading instruction—and the principles of EIR—come alive in their whole-group and small-group lessons. Chapters 3 and 4 look at excellent reading instruction through the lens of these EIR lessons. Chapter 6 discusses effective techniques for managing the reading block of instruction, including EIR lessons and independent work activities.

DISCUSS WITH YOUR COLLEAGUES

1. Discuss the stages of word recognition and describe the process of learning to read.

2. Share your current understandings about teaching reading. What was striking in this chapter? What changed your thinking?

3. When you consider implementing EIR, what are the challenges? What support systems are already in place in your school to lean on (parent volunteer programs, PTO, etc.)?

Meet the Teachers

● ●

The Differentiated Lessons and Teacher Collaboration That Support EIR

Choua Zhang, Stan Wolff, and Lena Jacobson, the teachers highlighted in this chapter, are connected to my work on effective instruction, school change in reading, and the EIR framework (Taylor 2010). Vignettes from their reading lessons are shared so that you can see how the teachers support and echo the reading content and pedagogy of EIR lessons. You'll read the teachers' own words as they share the benefits of engaging in professional development with colleagues. Struggling kindergartners will excel farther if you take on EIR as a group, whether you team up with teachers at your grade level, in the primary grades, or as a schoolwide initiative.

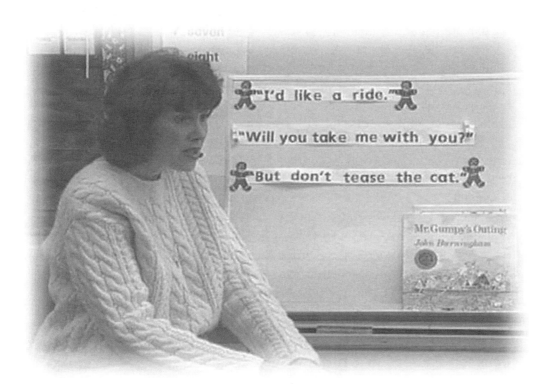

The three teachers in this chapter teach in different schools with different student populations and needs. Table 2–1 highlights this diversity.

Diversity in the Highlighted Teachers' Schools

Teacher	Years Teaching	School Setting	Percentage of Students Who Receive Subsidized Lunch	Percentage English Language Learners
Choua	14	Urban	93	87
Stan	10	Suburban	36	9
Lena	6	Rural	55	5

Table 2–1 Diversity in the Highlighted Teachers' Schools

The Teachers

Choua teaches at Adams Elementary, an inner-city school. The first languages of her students include Spanish, Somali, and Hmong. Choua has been teaching for fourteen years and participated in study groups (as part of a schoolwide reading improvement project) for three years, where she learned how to deliver EIR instruction (including follow-up support for students in need of more reading practice). During this three-year period, the students in Choua's class each year improved, on average, from the 18th to the 30th percentile on the Peabody Picture Vocabulary Test. In the spring, the students, on average, knew 50 letter names and 19 consonant sounds. They had a mean phonemic awareness score of 9 (if students score 6 or higher on this test, they are likely to succeed in learning to read in grade 1; Taylor 1991).

Stan teaches at Rossmoor Elementary, a suburban school. His ESL students are a relatively small percentage of the class and are primarily native Spanish speakers. Stan has been teaching for ten years, and he learned how to teach EIR lessons during his third year. During that year the students in his class, on average, went from the 43rd to 56th percentile on the Peabody Picture Vocabulary Test between fall and spring. In the spring, students on average knew 51 letter names and 20 consonant sounds. They had a mean phonemic awareness score of 9.

Lena teaches at Wheeler Elementary, a school in a rural area. She too has a low percentage of ESL students in her class. Lena has been teaching for six years, and she learned how to teach EIR lessons in the second year of her school's reading reform project. During that year, her class's reading scores, on average, improved from the 39th to the 52nd percentile on the Peabody Picture Vocabulary Test. In the spring, students on average knew 50 letter names and 19 consonant sounds. They had a mean phonemic awareness score of 10.

Common Factors in Students' Success

While these teachers have different styles and work in different settings, similarities in their instructional approach are instrumental to the success of their teaching and the reading achievement of their students.

When asked what components were critical to their success of her classroom reading program and the changes to her instruction that made it more effective, Choua mentioned she is more confident about:

- Using whole-group lessons to introduce strategies
- Facilitating small, flexible guided reading groups
- Supporting EIR small groups
- Creating rituals and routines
- Connecting letter sounds and guided sentence writing to the book they are reading
- Modeling what readers look like and sound like
- Monitoring oral language development and vocabulary
- Instilling a love of reading through enthusiasm
- Ensuring students experience lots of books and lots of genres; a quiet time to read

Stan listed these components:

- Balancing small groups, independent work
- Encouraging phonemic awareness and phonics, strategies for word recognition, interactive writing
- Focusing on comprehension and vocabulary; higher-level questions and higher-level responses; summarizing beginning-middle-end, character and setting, problem and solution
- Reading informational text in addition to fantasy
- Assessing in an informal, day-to-day way—seeing at a quick glance in students' journals the progress they have made in writing, reading, following directions, and working independently; keeping on top of what each child needs to know
- Planning purposeful lessons

Lena commented on these characteristics:

- Balancing small and large groups; creating opportunities for students to read and write independently; time for read-alouds and independent reading
- Differentiating instruction; using EIR to give kids who are struggling extra time on critical aspects of learning to read
- Modeling the reading process
- Using routines for phonemic awareness, letter sounds, guided reading and writing
- Expanding students' knowledge base and vocabulary
- Incorporating higher-level questions into lessons; teaching strategies for comprehension
- Choosing appropriate materials; using more engaging informational text than in the past
- Bonding with students; getting them motivated to read

All three teachers mention the importance of balancing whole-class, small-group, and independent learning; providing differentiated instruction; focusing on comprehension and vocabulary in addition to phonemic awareness and phonics; and using engaging materials. Choua and Lena specifically mention the importance of instilling the love of reading in their students and using EIR to support their struggling emergent readers.

Teacher Talk

I share the teacher quotes that follow to cheerlead you as you embark on learning to teach EIR lessons as one aspect of your classroom reading program. Whether you are a beginning or veteran teacher, the implementation of EIR will help your struggling readers make good growth in reading during their kindergarten year. Here's what Choua, Stan, and Lena had to say when I asked them how professional learning, including EIR, changed their instruction.

The Influence of Collaborative Professional Learning on Teaching Practice

CHOUA: Our weekly team meetings and monthly EIR study groups are really helpful, because we talk about the scope and sequence of what we will be teaching; we also talk about how each of our kids is doing and if he or she is ready to move on to the next step. I like to collaborate, and the EIR study groups have given us time to do this. I am a teacher who now works smarter, and I am 100 percent better with my interventions.

STAN: Professional learning within the school helps you see whether you are on the right track, affirms what you are doing, gives you ideas about what you should improve on. As a result, my awareness of my teaching and what I am doing and why has improved. I am more conscious of how I ask questions. I try to inform my students about what we are doing and why it helps them. I have learned how to provide student-driven instruction. I differentiate for every student in the classroom, challenging higher-ability students and providing scaffolds to help lower-ability students succeed.

LENA: The study groups are an excellent way to develop and reflect on instruction. The goal is to make all teachers the best they can be. The videos we share of our teaching are a good way to continue to grow, share ideas, and talk about ways to improve instruction—I get feedback on an actual lesson I have taught; this is about as real as it gets. Because of my professional development, I am much more aware of what I do, and I constantly modify my instruction based on what I learn. I emphasize higher-level questioning and vocabulary more than I did in the past. Our data retreats, when we look at the results of EIR, school, and district assessments, influence how I group children—who needs EIR intervention, who need more challenges and acceleration.

Biggest Benefits to Student Learning

When asked about their practices impacting student learning, again the teachers have similar responses.

CHOUA: Many students are reading! They are really putting letter sounds together and decoding words. They can retell the stories we read and they are also able to write about them. They are eager to use the vocabulary words we talk about. They are more challenged and there is a greater love for books. I believe these improvements are directly related to changes I have made in my teaching.

STAN: The biggest thing I see is that kids are reading sooner. I'm surprised how early my students can do things. My EIR students are getting a lot further, too. There have been improvements in all my students' comprehension and writing skills, compared with earlier years.

LENA: The kids are reading and writing at a higher level. They know how to use strategies and resources. We are doing much more with vocabulary, and the students seem to have broader vocabularies than in previous years. Also my kids, even those who struggle, have really become good writers this year. They are good at getting their ideas down on paper. I'm finding that if you give them support and keep at it, they can move forward. If you show it, model it, and practice it, they can do it.

Biggest Challenges

When asked about the biggest challenges, the teachers were honest about what they encountered.

CHOUA: Family-school partnerships are important, and we work hard at developing them. We send home book bags and weekly newsletters and make regular phone calls, always with some positive things to say. We also have family nights and, of course, conferences.

STAN: The varied levels of proficiency are a challenge. Also, keeping activities age appropriate and engaging takes work. Communication between parents and the school is important, and it is always a challenge to connect with parents in a useful way. Every Wednesday and Friday I have a parent come in and read their child's favorite stories. On Wednesday, Thursday, and Friday mornings, I have parent volunteers run a literacy station during our reading block.

LENA: Students coming in at so many different levels and with so many different exposures to literacy is a main challenge. Keeping students focused on what they are doing can be a challenge, but motivating activities help with that. Parents who read to their child at home every day help a lot.

On the following pages, detailed descriptions of these three teachers' reading lessons provide examples of what effective reading instruction looks like in practice. You will see how different teachers incorporate elements of effective reading instruction into their teaching based on their own styles and, of course, their students' needs. Notice how the teachers integrate the various components of content, including instruction in phonemic awareness, phonics, word recognition, vocabulary, and comprehension, as well as elements of pedagogy, including direct teaching and coaching; differentiation; and intellectually challenging independent, partner, and small-group activities.

The beauty of EIR is that it can be used in many different kinds of classrooms, complementing a reading workshop or any other balanced literacy instructional approach. As you read these lessons, remember they are overviews; they don't capture every teaching move but rather show how different teachers incorporate elements of effective reading instruction into their teaching based on their own styles and, of course, their students' needs.

Choua's reading block was described at the end of Chapter 1. Below are highlights from one of her reading lessons.

Summarizing Pages of an Informational Book, Writing Words in Sound Boxes, and Writing a Sentence About the Pages Read

Whole-Group Lesson

In this February EIR lesson, Choua and her students begin their day by quickly reviewing letter names and sounds on the alphabet chart. Then they continue reading a book about animal babies, reading a series of pages that tell how animals take care of and protect their young. As they read, Choua stops to talk about the meaning of unfamiliar but useful words as they come to them: "Monkeys spend a lot of time grooming their babies. What do you think *grooming* means?" When they read about how animals protect their babies, Choua explains what *protect* means. When they finish, Choua asks them to summarize the big ideas. With coaching as they look back at the pictures, they come up with "Mothers keep their babies clean." Choua asks them to share with a partner which animals do this, and then a few students share with the whole group ("Lions," "Baboons"). They move on to the next page and, with prompting, summarize, "Mothers move their babies." Examples they share with a partner and then in the whole group are elk, lions, and loons. Their summary of the final page they've read is, "Mothers watch their babies when they sleep." Examples they come up with from the pictures are elephants and whales.

Word Work Within the Whole-Group Lesson

Next, they fill in sound boxes for *cub* and *nap*. (Individual students have their own paper and do their own writing.) Choua begins, "I'm going to say some words from the story. See if you can tell me the words. Then we'll write them on our paper." Turning to the page about lions, she says, "What word is this on this page? /c/ /u/ /b/—yes, *cub*. Now let's put our finger on the number 1. What do you hear first in *cub*? Yes, /c/. In the first box next to the number 1 write the letter *c* which is the letter for the sound you hear first in *cub*—/c/ /u/ /b/, *cub*. What do you hear next in *cub*—/c/ /uuu/ /b/? Yes, short *u*. In the next box, write the letter *u* which is the letter for the middle sound you hear in /c/ /u/ /b/, *cub*. What sound do you hear at the end of cub? Yes, /b/. Does anyone know what letter makes this sound? Yes, *b*. In the last box write the letter *b*, which is the letter for the sound you hear at the end of cub /c/ /u/ /b/ cub."

Turning to the page about elephants, Choua gives the sounds /n/ /a/ /p/ and repeats the procedures.

She concludes the lesson by saying, "Let's read the two words we wrote. Put your finger by box number one of the first word. Run your finger under each sound like this as we say the word—/c/ /u/ /b/. Now let's do the same thing for the next word—/n/ /a/ /p/."

Independent Follow-Up Work

At the end of the whole-group lesson, Choua sends most students off to write a sentence about the book on baby animals and draw a picture. They can write about the mother lion, baboon, elk, elephant, or whale as she cleans, moves, or watches her baby. Choua gives them a sheet that has the sentence partially completed: *The mother* _____ _____ *her baby.* When students finish the sentence, they are to move on to their individual book bins. In the book bins are many picture books that they have read together as a class, along with other books at each student's reading level. Students are to "read" through some books on their own, add two books to their reading log, and pick a favorite book to "read" and talk about with a partner. Choua will also be calling each small group up for a lesson at their reading level. A teaching assistant arrives at the end of the whole-group lesson to work with students at their desks.

Small-Group Work for Students Who Need More Support

Choua then works with the EIR target group at the reading table. They repeat some of activities they just did in the whole-group lesson. They orally summarize the page about mothers grooming their young; Choua helps them write one of the sound box words again; and she helps them complete their sentence about the book that the other students are working on at their seats.

Summary/Analysis

In this lesson, Choua provides excellent, differentiated instruction as she teaches the comprehension strategy of summarizing with the whole group, then reinforces this strategy with a small group of students who need more support. Her instruction is intellectually challenging, students' independent activities are motivating and require high-level thinking, and students are actively engaged.

Partner Work

While some teachers choose partners randomly, others are more deliberate, pairing students who will be able to support each other. Switching partners every two or three weeks also works well. This way, students experience working with different types of learners.

High-Level Talk About a Story, Interactive Writing, and the Comprehension Strategies of Making Connections and Summarizing Narrative Text

Stan has a 115-minute reading block. He begins with a 25-minute whole-group lesson that is based on his school's core reading program. After a 5-minute transition, he spends about an hour working with three guided reading groups. During 5-minute transitions between groups he checks on students' independent work. He has an educational assistant in his classroom to help students who are working independently.

Typically, after lunch he spends 15 minutes on an EIR whole-group lesson, followed by 10 minutes on an EIR follow-up lesson (a second dose of quality, small-group instruction for his struggling readers). During the small-group lesson, other students complete activities from the morning reading block or read independently.

Whole-Group Lesson

Stan tells his students, who are at their seats, that they are going to write interactively about the story they read the day before. He gives each student a sheet of paper and offers a card-size alphabet chart to students who want one. "Yesterday we read the story *Are You There, Baby Bear?* Good readers make connections to their life. Good readers take time to think about what they read and relate it to something in their life or something they know. This helps them understand what they read. In the story *Are You There, Baby Bear?* would you have done what Alfie did? Why or why not? Pause and think."

A student responds, "He thought that his brothers and sisters came through the woods."

Stan asks, "Have you ever waited for a baby brother or sister?" Some students say they have. "How did it make you feel?"

Students say it made them feel happy. To get them to say more, Stan has students turn to the person next to them and tell about a time they waited for something. Then Stan asks one student to share.

She says, "I waited for a baby."

Stan prompts the student to elaborate: "How did you feel?"

"Happy."

"Why did you want the baby to come?"

"So I could love it."

Stan continues the lesson. "We didn't have time to write about the story yesterday, so today we will. The purpose today is to learn to be good writers, because that will help us be better readers. I am going to model how you write from left to right just as you go from the left to the right when you read."

Stan has them clap the number of words in the sentence, *He saw the baby bear.* Then he asks, "What letter do we write for the sound we hear first in *he*?" Students say the letter *h*. Stan prints the letter on his sheet as the students print on their sheet. "What do we hear at the end of /h/ /e/? Yes, we hear long *e* and the letter is *e*." Stan circulates as the students write the word. He reminds them to leave a space after the words.

Next, he says the word *saw,* and asks the students what sound they hear at the beginning and what letter they should write that makes this sound. They say /s/ and the letter *s*. Stan tells them the word ends with the letters *a* and *w*, and they finish writing it.

They all write the word *the,* a basic sight word on their word wall. Then Stan asks, "What word from our sentence are we doing now?" Students say *baby.* Since they are running short on time, he spells *baby* for them and they copy down the letters. He asks them how they would start to spell *bear,* and they say *b*. He continues, "The middle is tricky, so I'll tell you, it's *ea*. Now, what do you hear at the end of *bear*?" They say *r*. "Okay, turn to your partner and tell them why you put a period at the end of the sentence." A student shares his idea. "If you didn't have a period, you wouldn't stop."

Stan and his students read the sentence chorally, and he tells them that later, while he is working with small groups, he wants them to draw a picture on the back of their paper of something they remember about the story, share their picture with a partner, and also reread their group sentence with their partner.

Whole-Group EIR Lesson

The students then move to the circle and Stan reads *The Little Red Hen.* He stops to talk briefly about the meaning of some useful but unfamiliar words. He also talks about strategies for reading: "Good readers make connections when they read. If you were the little red hen what would you have done if the animals didn't help you or if you asked your friends and they didn't help you? Turn to a neighbor and tell how you would feel if you were the little red hen."

A student says, "I would feel sad."

Stan agrees. "I would feel sad, too. Have you ever asked anyone to help you and they wouldn't help you? How about zipping your jacket or putting on your boots? Share with a partner." They do.

Stan continues, "Good readers summarize. That is a strategy we use when we talk about the story and it helps us remember the story. We remember the most important ideas from the story so it helps us understand." Stan tells them that in a little while they will each write words and draw pictures to tell what *The Little Red Hen* is about—beginning, middle, and end. But first, he talks about it with them.

"What did she do in the beginning?"

A student says, "She picked up the seeds."

"What happened in the middle?"

A student says, "Her friends did not help her."

Stan prompts, "What did they do?"

"They were sleeping."

"Playing."

Stan asks, "What does she tell them at the end?"

A student answers, "She only lets the people eat who helped her."

The students have talked about the author's message before, so when Stan asks, "What is the author's message?" a student quickly replies, "You should help other people." Stan tells them they will all be working hard like the little red hen. When they are done with their summary and their picture about *Are You There, Baby Bear?* they are to read from their book boxes and write in their journal about one of their books. The students return to their desks, and the instructional assistant helps them as needed.

Small-Group Lesson with Above-Average Readers

Stan begins to work with a group of six students who are already reading simple texts. He gives each student a copy of *The Dig*. He asks them to look at the pictures and predict what the book will be about. One student says, "It looks like they will be digging for a treasure." They read the story chorally as Stan coaches, "I noticed you had trouble with the word *dig*. What if you didn't have pictures, how could you figure out the word?" A student says, "Sound out the word." Stan says, "Good, you could segment and blend /d/ /i/ /g/. Let's go on. This is a fun book."

Stan gives the students a sheet with sound boxes on it. The first word he asks them to write is *map*. He has them sound out the word and write the letters for the sounds in the boxes. (He doesn't help them as much as he did during the whole-group lesson.) Then he shows them how he wrote the letters on his sheet so they can check their work. He tells them the next word to sound out is *dig*. Students say the word and write the letters in the sound boxes. Stan continues, "The next word is *have*. Sound it out by yourself." He tells them that the *e* on the end is silent. Then he tells them to write the sentence *I have a map* on their own on the bottom of their sound box sheet. "Next, I want you to write the sentence *I like to dig*. Good job, you remembered the period." Stan has the students read the sentences on their sheet before returning to their seats. At their seats students are to reread their guided reading book and use a narrative summary sheet to summarize the story.

Summary/Analysis

In the whole-group lessons, Stan challenges his students with high-level questions and guides them in writing sentences about a story they have read the day before. He then asks them to summarize a story they have also read earlier (a comprehension strategy). For independent work, he challenges his students with motivating activities: they draw a picture about *Are You There, Baby Bear?*, reread the group sentences with a partner, summarize *The Little Red Hen* in words and pictures, and read from their book boxes. His advanced students are already able to read on their own, and he coaches them as they take the lead in reading their story.

High-Level Talk and Summarizing Informational Text

Lena has a 115-minute reading block each day. She begins with a 25-minute whole-group lesson from her basal reading program. She then spends about an hour with three guided reading groups. She has a 15-minute EIR lesson and after lunch, a 10-minute small EIR group. During small group lessons, the other students work independently or read for pleasure from books of their own choosing. Lena has an educational assistant in her room to help the students who are working independently, as well as an ELL teacher who works with two small groups of English language learners.

Whole-Group Lesson

Lena reads an informational book on penguins. "Today our book is called *Penguin Rescue. Rescue* is a good word for us to know. Do you know what it means?"

A student answers, "It means to save someone who is in danger."

Lena gives an example of when she rescued something and when someone rescued her. "Let's see if you can think of a time when you rescued someone or when someone rescued you. Or maybe you heard of someone on TV or saw in a book when someone was rescued."

Students "think, pair, and share." Lena circulates and listens to various conversations. She calls on a few students to share with the class. One student says, "When I was three years old, I was climbing down a mountain and I slipped. My mom grabbed my hand to help me." Lena coaches the student to use the new word, "So what did she do?" She points to the word written on the board. The student answers, "She rescued me."

Lena continues, "After we read, we're going to practice our strategy of making a summary of an information book. I'm going to ask you, *What is this book about?* Any time you read a book, you can make a summary of what the book was about to help you understand the most important ideas." Lena opens the book, begins reading, and stops to tell what *oil* is and what it's used for. She continues to read aloud and stops to ask a question. "Think about that a minute. Why do you think the penguins would die if they're all covered with oil?"

Students "think, pair, and share" as Lena listens. A few students take turns sharing their ideas with the group. One student says, "They might die because the oil might sink into their bodies."

Lena prompts the student to elaborate, "And why could that make them die?"

"Because they couldn't get anymore fish."

"The oil might sink into their feathers and get into their heart."

Lena clarifies, "Another reason is—remember penguins can't fly. They can only swim. If they have oil in their feathers, they can't stay warm, swim, or catch food."

Lena continues reading and points out in a picture how people put sweaters on the penguins and fed them. "Now, if you were some of those workers, how would you feel about what you had done?"

Students say they'd feel happy.

Lena prompts them to elaborate: "Why would you feel happy?"

A student says, "Because they were sad."

Lena elaborates, "Because you saved their lives, right? You rescued them."

A student adds, "They felt happy. And when they were covered in oil, if they would die, there wouldn't be any of those animals left on earth. Just like dinosaurs."

Lena responds, "You made a neat connection, because if these penguins didn't survive, that whole type of penguin would have become extinct. What message do you think the author is trying to give us?"

"That you can help out animals that need it. You need to be careful."

Lena prompts, "Tell me more about that."

"The ship driver should have tried not to hit the rock. Then the oil wouldn't have spilled and hurt the penguins."

After this high-level discussion, Lena returns to the task of summarizing. "Let's go back to our summary. What's it about?"

A student answers, "It's about penguins and how they got rescued from oil."

"Good, and you can tell someone at home about this book today by summarizing like this."

Small-Group Lesson

Students move to their work areas. Lena sits with a group of five. "We've been talking about what makes a good summary. What's a summary?"

A student says, "It tells what the story is about."

Lena continues, "Today we're going to let you practice making a summary when we read the book *Legs*, which we read together yesterday." She hands a whiteboard to each student. "But we're going to start out by doing some word work. I'd like you to think about some sounds you hear in this word and write it at the top." Lena slowly sounds out *leg*.

Students write the word while Lena writes the word on her whiteboard. One student writes *lag*. Lena sounds out what he wrote and then sounds out *leg*. "What sound do we need in the middle of that word? The student says *e* and fixes his word.

"Now we're going to write *peg*." Lena sounds it out. Students and Lena write the word on their whiteboard. Next they sound out and spell *pet* and *let*. Lena says, "Look at all of your words and see if there's anything alike about all the words."

A student says, "They all have *e*."

"Yes, they all have the /eh/ sound. I also see that many of the words have *eg* or *et* at the end." Lena circles these letter combinations in each of the words on her board. Students do the same. Lena holds up a chart on word-recognition strategies. "That's a strategy we use for figuring out words we don't know. It's called looking for chunks. If we see a word that has *et* or *eg* at the end, we can just add the beginning sound and figure out the word, like this, /l/ /eg/, *leg*." Lena collects the whiteboards.

"Now when we read our book about legs, we'll think about the summary we'll make at the end. You can start trying to read this book on your own. If you get stuck on a word, think about the strategies you can use to figure it out." She points to the chart.

Students read aloud at their own pace. Lena listens and coaches them to use word-recognition strategies as they go. "This is a hard word to sound out. Maybe the chart might help." The students figure out zero. Lena, says, "All right, *zero* means none. Do you think it would be better to have zero legs or two legs?"

A student answers, "Two legs."

"Why?"

"Because you can get more places faster."

Another student says, "I think zero would be better."

"Why?"

"Because I think it would be fun to slither on the ground."

Next Lena has students read a page in unison with her and asks, "How do we know that word is *beetle*, not *bug*?"

A student says, "Because it has an *e* sound in it and *bug* would have an *uh* sound in it."

Lena elaborates, "And it's a longer word than *bug*, isn't it?" They finish reading the page in unison. One student exclaims, "I don't ever want to see that bug!"

Lena moves on. "Now we need to think about the summary. Think about what this book is about. We are going to fill in a sentence about our summary." Lena hands each student a sheet that says, *This book is about* _____. "Does anybody know what the first part of the sentence says?" A student reads the words aloud. "Are we going to write everything this story is about?"

A student answers, "Just the most important part."

"What is the whole book about?"

Students say legs.

"Yes, it's about legs. Can you go a little further than that? What about legs? Whose legs?"

Students say animal legs.

"Can you still go a little further?"

"How many legs animals have."

"Good job. Let's write, *This book is about how many legs animals have.*" Lena writes the words on a whiteboard, sounding out the word *animal* letter-by-letter and having the students identify the letter that goes with each sound. The students write the sentence on their own papers. Lena reminds them to leave a finger space between words. Finally they read the sentence in unison. Lena says, "When you go home today, can you tell someone the summary of the books you read today?"

Students say they can.

"We made a summary of what this book is about. You can do this any time you are reading. You do this by telling the most important part of the story."

Summary/Analysis

Lena teaches a comprehension strategy to the whole-group lesson and follows up in a guided reading group. She also coaches emergent readers in word-recognition strategies as they read decodable texts that nevertheless contain some words that they need to figure out. These kindergartners come up with fascinating ideas that show they are really thinking about the books they are reading.

In Chapter 6, we return to the teachers' classrooms. We revisit their daily reading schedules that include the EIR lessons they provide to their students who need more support. We also learn about the motivating, independent learning activities they set up for their students to engage in as they work with guided reading and EIR groups.

Making a Schoolwide Commitment to Kindergarten Emergent Readers

Take a moment to think about your own school, and how you might collaborate with one or more of your colleagues to implement EIR within a shared vision of effective reading instruction.

The best teaching takes place in schools in which teachers develop a shared set of understandings and beliefs about teaching and learning in general and about teaching reading in particular. Considerable research in the past decade has identified the following characteristics of schoolwide reading programs that support teachers' abilities to increase students' reading abilities. These schools have:

▶ a unified vision for teaching reading in every grade and a cohesive schoolwide program (Taylor, Raphael, and Au 2010; Taylor et al. 2005)

▶ a substantial number of minutes and designated blocks of time devoted to reading instruction in every grade (Taylor et al. 2000)

▶ a schoolwide assessment plan in which student data are collected and used regularly to inform instruction (Pressley et al. 2003; Taylor et al. 2000; Taylor et al. 2002)

▶ interventions in place to meet the students' needs who are experiencing reading difficulties, who have special needs, and who are English language learners (Foorman and Torgesen 2001; Mathes et al. 2005; Taylor et al. 2000)

▶ effective parent partnerships (Edwards 2004; Taylor et al. 2002)

An individual teacher working hard on her own to enhance her practice can make a huge difference in the lives of the students in her class. And yet, it is ideal to have an effective schoolwide reading program in place, whereby a common vision, time to work together, and a culture of peer support are part of your school's DNA. As Choua, Stan, Lena, and so many other teachers attest, working with colleagues can provide amazing support. It's hard to examine and critique your own practice. Trusted colleagues can watch you teach, give you feedback, point out your strengths, and offer ideas to enhance your instruction. This support helps you look closely at your practice, make modifications, and in the end teach as effectively as possible so all your students become skilled, motivated readers.

I hope that you carry this overview of effective reading instruction with you as you read about EIR strategies in the next chapter. You might also want to explore the content, pedagogy, and interpersonal skills of exemplary teachers further. Professional books and research articles abound on many of the components of effective reading instruction discussed in Chapters 1 and 2. (Also see pages in the endmatter for Recommended Professional Readings.)

DISCUSS WITH YOUR COLLEAGUES

1. Discuss each of the three teachers described in this chapter. What do you like about their lessons? What questions do you have? As a group, is there one strand of effective reading instruction you would like to explore more?

2. Discuss instructional ideas you might try after reading about Choua, Stan, and Lena.

The Weekly Lesson Routine

Now it's time to look at the daily EIR lessons, the rational behind the various components, and some basic getting started information. The EIR kindergarten program, like the other EIR programs, is supplemental instruction designed to accelerate children's literacy learning. The goal of the program is to develop children's oral language, phonemic awareness, and emergent literacy abilities through literature-based activities and to have them leave kindergarten with the skills needed to learn to read in grade 1.

Ideally, the EIR kindergarten program is used with the entire class for between 10 and 15 minutes a day. If you do not finish an activity you start on one day, such as word work that involves children writing words or sentences, you can finish the next day when the whole group meets again. Through the program, all students develop their oral language and vocabulary abilities, phonemic awareness, phonics knowledge and decoding abilities, print concept awareness, and story comprehension. The more capable children become models for the children who are less skilled.

Additionally, an important component of the program involves providing supplemental help to the children who are having difficulty with literacy concepts and skills. Each day the goal is to spend between 5 and 10 minutes with these students going over, or perhaps completing, some of the activities that were covered with the entire class. Some of the same discussion questions are asked again, and the activities the children had the most difficulty with are repeated. Ideally, groups should be limited to four or five students so all group members get a chance to participate.

First, let's review a few foundational ideas:

▌ With EIR, students' emergent reading progress is accelerated because your instruction is based on the same effective reading instruction you use with *all* students—this is not remediation.

▌ Students who are struggling with emergent reading get an extra shot of quality, small-group reading instruction. These children are getting this support in addition to, not instead of, other whole-group, small-group, and one-on-one attention.

▌ The lessons feature engaging children's books. (See Table 3–1 here and on the DVD for a list of exemplar books for the kindergarten program.)

Children who struggle in kindergarten with letter names, letter sounds, phonemic awareness, and oral language development get the help they need and are likely to become independent readers in first grade.

Table 3–1 Kindergarten Exemplar Book Titles

Book Title	Author
The 20th Century Children's Poetry Treasury	Jack Prelutsky
Babar's ABC	Laurent de Brunhoff
Go, Dog. Go!	P. D. Eastman
Over in the Meadow	Ezra Jack Keats
The Little Panda	Harley Chan
What Game Shall We Play?	Pat Hutchins
Mr. Gumpy's Outing	John Burningham
Usborne Farmyard Tales Alphabet Book	Heather Amery and Stephen Cartwright
Good-Night, Owl!	Pat Hutchins
I Know an Old Lady	Nadine Westcott
Signs on the Way	Marvin Buckley
A, My Name Is Alice	Jane Bayer
The Three Billy Goats Gruff	Paul Galdone
Hattie and the Fox	Mem Fox
Are You My Mother?	P. D. Eastman
Peanut Butter and Jelly	Nadine Westcott
Do Like Kyla	Angela Johnson
The Mitten	Alvin Tresselt

Time to Sleep	Denise Fleming
Jump, Frog, Jump!	Robert Kalan
Whistle for Willie	Ezra Jack Keats
A Bird Flies By	Marilyn Woolley
Good Morning, Chick	Mirra Ginsburg
Jamaica Tag-Along	Juanita Havill
Just Grandpa and Me	Mercer Mayer
Jamaica and Briana	Juanita Havill
The Little Red Hen	Paul Galdone
Wild Bears	Seymour Simon
Ant	Karen Hartley and Chris Macro
What Animals Need	James Nguyen
Caterpillar	Karen Hartley, Chris Macro, and Philip Taylor

Table 3–1 Kindergarten Exemplar Book Titles

Getting Started: FAQs

Chapter 5 provides more information on determining which children might benefit from the additional EIR small-group support. For now, here are some questions teachers commonly ask about setting up the groups.

How many students are in an EIR group targeted for extra support?

Each group should have four or five students (six at most). If there are more than six children in your room who need the additional EIR lessons, I would recommend finding a way to have two groups instead of just one. If you have Title 1 at your school, perhaps the Title 1 teacher can take one group and you can take the other. (Periodically switch groups so you have a sense of the strengths and weaknesses of all your readers who need additional support to become successful.)

How should I form the extra-support groups if I need to have two of them?

It's a good idea to put the faster-progressing students in one group and the slower-progressing students in the other, so all students will learn at about the same pace. The faster-moving students won't call out answers at the expense of the slower-moving students, and the slower-moving students won't be discouraged when the faster-moving students catch on more quickly. (Students in the faster-progressing group may be pulled from the group as soon as they catch up with the rest of the class. Guidelines to help you decide whether a child no longer needs small-group EIR lessons are provided in Chapter 5.)

Who should teach the EIR students targeted for extra support?

As hard as it is to teach two EIR groups, should you find you need to do this, I cannot recommend that an instructional aide teach one of the groups. Children at risk of reading failure desperately need quality, supplemental reading instruction, provided by certified teachers, in addition to the regular reading program. Also, the whole group EIR lessons should be taught by a certified teacher as well.

What advice do you have regarding English language learners and EIR?

Many ELLs, especially children such as Hmong students whose first language sounds are very different from English, will have more difficulty with the phonemic awareness activities than native English speakers. Nevertheless, put them in a small group to practice EIR activities in the fall unless they have the opportunity to learn to read in their first language. You do not want to take the chance of preventing any student from learning to read by postponing their participation in small-group practice sessions on EIR lessons to a later time, such as after the first of the year. Also, I have found that ELLs generally do well in EIR (Taylor 2001).

How do special education students fare with EIR?

I have also found that EIR works well with students who have learning disabilities. No modifications to the program are recommended. Students who are developmentally and cognitively delayed should participate in the whole-class EIR lessons, but they will need additional one-on-one attention to feel successful.

Do the children in EIR groups feel stigmatized?

Over the many years I've been researching and implementing EIR, teachers report that children do not feel stigmatized. In fact, children love the fast pace and interesting texts, and their feelings of success are enhanced when they have the opportunity to revisit activities from the whole-class EIR lessons in a small-group setting. All children are in small groups with their teacher, so no one seems to thinks much about who is with the teacher when. But the children in EIR lessons like the extra time with the teacher if she is the one teaching the EIR group.

What is the optimum time of the year to start EIR?

It is best to begin EIR in September or October. However, if you have just bought or been given this book and it is February, then February is the best time! In February, begin with the week 12–15 lessons (if these lessons are too challenging, drop back to week 9 or 10). One of the major problems I've discovered in the hundreds of kindergarten classrooms I have visited over the past twenty years is that the students, especially the struggling readers, are presented with literacy activities that are too easy for them and repeat these activities more times than necessary. The point of EIR is to challenge students and accelerate their development of emergent literacy, oral language, and vocabulary abilities as well as foster their enjoyment of good literature.

What is the best way for me to be confident about teaching EIR lessons?

First read the summary of weekly procedures in Figure 3–1, then read the detailed lesson routines and watch the corresponding video clips on the accompanying DVD. (These components are described in greater detail in Chapter 4 in the context of weekly lessons.) Soon, the EIR routines will seem very natural, and, as many teachers have reported, you will feel that the extra work on your part is worth the effort! For the past fifteen years, I have consistently found that teachers, by February, are very excited about the progress their struggling readers are making.

How do I know when I am ready to teach the lessons?

Even after reading this book, you may not feel ready to conduct the lessons. Nevertheless, the best way to learn EIR procedures is to jump in and try them. If (when!) you have questions, reread parts of the book or rewatch particular video clips. Ideally, you will be working with a group of colleagues who are also learning and implementing EIR, and you can share successes and discuss questions and uncertainties together.

Weekly Lesson Plans and Routines

Although the EIR programs for grades 1–5 center around a three- to-five-day routine, the kindergarten program has twenty-seven specific weekly lesson plans that you can easily get through during the school year. (It's important to keep on schedule, since some of the most essential activities are covered in the last one-third of the program.) Each weekly plan is built around two or three books in the context of which children enjoy literature and respond to it creatively, develop their vocabulary, make connections to their lives, and participate in a carefully designed scope and sequence of phonemic awareness and other emergent literacy activities. Figure 3–1, which is also on the DVD, summarizes this scope and sequence.

You should approach these phonemic awareness and emergent literacy activities from the perspective of exposure, not mastery—that is, don't expect children to master them. By being exposed to these skills, children will be further along in their literacy development and consequently more ready to learn to read in grade 1.

The remainder of this chapter provides an overview of the literacy activities in the program, especially those that develop phonemic awareness (video clips of kindergarten teachers using these lessons with their students are provided on the DVD). Chapter 4 includes a complete sample lesson for each literacy

Scope and Sequence of EIR Emergent Literacy Activities in Kindergarten

Fall Lessons
  Weeks 1–5   September–October
  Weeks 6–8   November
  Weeks 9–11   December

Winter Lessons
  Weeks 12–15   January
  Weeks 16–18   February

Spring Lessons
  Weeks 19–21   March
  Weeks 22–24   April
  Weeks 25–27   May

Introduction of Emergent Literacy Skills or Activities

Week 1
▶ Discuss texts, explore new vocabulary and concepts, act out text
▶ Identify letters A–L

Week 2
▶ Identify letters M–Z

Week 3
▶ Identify and produce rhyming words

Week 4
▶ Identify (hear number of) words in a sentence
▶ Observe as teacher points to each word while reading a story summary
▶ Develop understanding that readers read left to right, with a return sweep to the next line

Week 6*
▶ Hear and segment the beginning sound in a word
▶ Identify pictures of things that begin with the sounds for the letters A–H

Week 7
▶ Identify pictures of things or words that begin with the sounds for I–R

Week 8
▶ Identify pictures of things or words that begin the sounds for S–Z

Week 9
▶ Hear the beginning and ending sound in a word
▶ Identify and write (or trace) lower- and uppercase A, B, C, D
▶ Develop letter-sound correspondences A, B, C, D

*No new activities introduced in weeks 5, 15, 23, 24, 26, and 27.

Figure 3–1 Scope and Sequence of EIR Emergent Literacy Activities in Kindergarten (continues)

Week 10
) Hear and segment the ending sound of a word
) Identify and write (or trace) lower- and uppercase E, F, G, H
) Develop letter-sound correspondences E, F, G, H

Week 11
) Segment the sounds in words with two phonemes (consonant-vowel or vowel-consonant)
) Identify and write (or trace) lower- and uppercase I, J, K, L
) Develop letter-sound correspondences I, J, K, L

Week 12
) Identify and write (or trace) lower- and uppercase M, N, O, P
) Develop letter-sound correspondences M, N, O, P

Week 13
) Segment the sounds in three-phoneme words
) Identify and write (or trace) lower- and uppercase Q, R, S, T
) Develop letter-sound correspondences Q[U], R, S, T

Week 14
) Identify and write (or trace) lower- and uppercase letters U, V, W, X, Y, Z
) Develop letter-sound correspondences U, V, W, X, Y, Z

Week 16*
) Engage in interactive sentence writing
) Blend two phonemes to make a word in an oral sentence

Week 17
) Say words by blending three phonemes pronounced by teacher as she is reading
) Summarize a narrative by engaging in interactive sentence writing

Week 18
) Say three-letter words from the story by blending the phonemes pronounced by the teacher in isolation (after reading)

Week 19
) Point to, say, and blend three letters in sound boxes that represent the phonemes of a word

Week 20
) Write letters of three-phoneme words in sound boxes

Week 21
) Hear the two parts in two-syllable words
) Summarize an informational text by engaging in interactive sentence writing

Week 22
) Track print while reading, pointing to each word as it is read and not confusing two-syllable words for two words

Week 25
) For a consonant-vowel-consonant word from the story, write more words that belong to same word family

No new activities introduced in weeks 5, 15, 23, 24, 26, and 27.

Figure 3–1 Scope and Sequence of EIR Emergent Literacy Activities in Kindergarten (continued)

activity when it is introduced for the first time. The DVD contains complete weekly lessons for all the exemplar books so you can see the kinds of learning activities you need to provide. However, you can present the activities to your students using your own favorite books.

Teachers have told me they needed to pay careful attention to their timing to get through the recommended daily activities in 10 minutes (or 15 minutes initially). I always tell teachers that if they take longer than 15 minutes for the whole-class lesson and 10 minutes for small-group practice for students who need more support, they may be tempted to drop EIR because it seems to take up too much time. So try to stay within the 20- to 25-minute time frame.

Overview of the Lesson Components

Text Discussion

Every week, opportunities are provided for discussion in which children must think about the story or informational text and questions you ask, and then express themselves. We know from the research literature (Adams 1990; Snow et al. 1998) that not only is reading aloud to children important, but the verbal interaction that goes along with the reading of the story is also important. Furthermore, we know that oral language ability at the beginning of first grade is a powerful predictor of reading and writing ability by the end of the elementary grades (Adams 1990; NRP 2000; Stahl 2001).

Prompt students to think about the meaning of the book you are reading by asking high-level questions as or after you read it. (Examples are provided in Figure 3–2 and on the DVD.) High-level questions get the children to think about and interpret the story. They're not answered with a yes or a no. High-level questions may also prompt students to connect the meaning of the story to their own lives (see the examples in Figure 3–3).

You will need to model by giving example answers to the higher-level questions you ask. You will also have to regularly coach students to elaborate on their answers or model doing so by turning their one- or two-word answers into complete sentences (especially with ELLs). Nevertheless, it is important that you expect your kindergartners to think and to be capable of this level of response. The payoff is worth it! Teachers who ask students to respond to higher-level questions about what they have read see greater growth in students' reading scores than teachers who don't (Taylor et al. 2003, 2005). To ensure that each child understands the story well enough to participate in the higher-level discussion and to develop students' vocabulary, briefly discuss the meaning of potentially unfamiliar but useful words as you read aloud.

Typically, have students turn to a partner and share answers to the questions you ask while you listen to what the pairs are saying. Then call on one or two students to share their ideas with the larger group. It is important to give the children enough time to respond when you call on them. Explain that you will not be able to call on everyone with an idea but that everyone will get a chance to share ideas during the week. (For every verbal child you call on, give a less verbal child a chance to respond as well.)

Coaching for Comprehension:
Questions and Prompts for Teachers

Interpretive Questions Based on the Text

▶ What kind of person do you think [*name of character*] is? What in the story makes you think this?

▶ What are some good [*bad*] things that happen in the story? Why do you think these are good [*bad*] things?

▶ What was a problem in the story? How was the problem solved?

▶ What do you think is an important thing that happened in the story? Why do you think it is important?

▶ Why do you think the author gave the title he/she did to the story?

▶ What did you like best about [*name of character*]? Why? What in the story helped you feel this way?

▶ What did you not like about [*name of character*]? Why? What in the story made you feel this way?

▶ Would you have done the same things the main character did? Why or why not? What might you have done differently?

▶ Why do you think [*character in the story*] did [*an action in the story*]?

▶ How did [*character in the story*] change? Why do you think this happened?

▶ What happened in the beginning [*the middle*] [*the end*] of the story?

▶ What did you learn from this story?

▶ What important ideas can we learn from this informational text?

High-Level Questions Relating a Story Concept to Children's Lives

▶ Which character is most like you? Why?

▶ Which character would you like to be like? Why?

▶ Which character would you like to have as a friend? What in the story helped you make this decision?

▶ How are you like [*character in the story*]? How are you different?

▶ Can you compare anything in this story to [*another story*] [*something you have done in your classroom*]? Why do you think these are alike or different?

▶ Could you find these animals [*events*] in [*your state*]? Why or why not? Where? What might happen if they were in [*your state*]?)

▶ What did you like about this story? Why?

Figure 3–2 Coaching for Comprehension: Questions and Prompts for Teachers

Story Discussion Questions That Relate to Students' Lives

Good-Night Owl!—Have you ever had trouble sleeping like the animals did at the end of the story? What kept you from sleeping? How did you finally fall asleep?

I Know an Old Lady—Have you ever swallowed something by mistake like the old lady did? Think first and then tell your partner about it.

Do Like Kyla—Do you have an older brother, sister, cousin, or neighbor you like to do things with? What things do you do and why do you like to do things with this person? Share your ideas with your partner.

Figure 3–3 Story Discussion Questions That Relate to Students' Lives

see it in Action

Talking About Text

Paula Berger is reading *Just Grandpa and Me*, by Mercer Mayer, with her kindergarten class in the spring. After they read, she asks students to think before they share about a time they got to do something special with a member of their family. She calls on a few students. One boy starts out, "I went out with my grampa . . ." and can't think of anything more to say. Paula coaches, "Where did you go? What did you do?" A girl who is more verbal briefly tells about a trip to the zoo with her grandparents. Then Paula asks everyone to share their ideas with a partner as she coaches a group close to her. She keeps this part of the activity brief, giving them about 30 seconds to share.

Time is limited during EIR lessons; you won't have time for all students to answer your question. Let one or two children answer, and explain to the others that you will call on them in the next day or two. Even though you would normally have several more children respond, students easily adapt. Also, keep reminding yourself that wait time is important. Wait at least three seconds after asking your question.

Vocabulary and Concepts

Ask questions about concepts (colors, opposites, feelings, body parts, etc.) as they come up in the poems and stories you are reading. Also talk about the meaning of words that you believe many students will not know, especially those they will find useful in many contexts, at the point they are encountered in the poems and stories you are reading (Beck and McKeown 2001; Beck et al. 2002). Discuss the most important words again after you have finished reading.

Creative Dramatics

Creative dramatics provide a safe medium in which students can express themselves. Have all children make story-related movements as you read aloud to them, or assign roles and let specific children act out/speak relevant parts as you reread or retell the story. This is a way to help children become comfortable speaking in front of a group. It's also fun and doesn't require any prompts. Children's wonderful imaginations will carry them through the retelling of all or a part of a story. At first, you'll be the narrator. Later, have children take turns filling this role, supporting them as necessary.

See it iN ActioN

Acting Out a Story

Nancy Sharp and her students reread and act out *Mr. Gumpy's Outing*. The students say they know this story, and Nancy says, "But today we are going to talk more about the story and act it out." Nancy and her students retell the story as she asks questions and they look at pictures in the book. As they reread the story, she asks them to tell her some of the words. She asks them again what *squabble* means. Then, they all get up to show her how to *trample*. Nancy then asks for volunteers. As Nancy retells different parts of the story, they act it out, saying some of the lines. Afterward, they have a brief discussion about boat safety.

Nancy uses some simple props: a large sheet of paper for the boat, a kettle for the tea party at the end, a fishing hat for Mr. Gumpy. Elaborate props like the animal faces aren't necessary. The little girl with the wooly shawl was happy with her prop that "turned her into a sheep." Children are good at using their imaginations without any props at all.

Nancy adds a nice touch by concluding with a brief discussion about the story and boat safety.

tip

Work on segmenting phonemes in words so you voice the sounds as crisply as possible. Especially try to avoid adding a prolonged /uh/ to a consonant with a "stop" sound (/b/, /c/, /d/, /g/, /h/, /j/, /k/, p/, /q/, /t/). Admittedly, this isn't easy, but you'll get better with practice. For example instead of /kuh/ /ah/ /tuh/, say /k/ /a/ /t/.

Phonemic Awareness

Many different kinds of activities to promote phonemic awareness are provided in instructional materials you purchase. However, research has found that the two best predictors of end-of-first-grade reading ability are phonemic segmentation (hearing the sounds in a word) and phonemic blending (blending the sounds in a word to pronounce it) (Adams 1991; NRP 2000; Taylor 1998). Therefore, EIR in kindergarten focuses on phonemic segmentation followed by phonemic blending. Research on a sequence of instructional activities to develop children's phonemic awareness in kindergarten or early first grade supports this progression (Taylor 1998).

In week 3 you identify rhyme, an important precursor to the development of phonemic segmentation and blending ability. In weeks 6–8, you focus on hearing the beginning sounds in words. In weeks 9–11, you focus on hearing the beginning and ending sounds in words. In weeks 13–15, you work with the children on segmenting the sounds in two- and then three-phoneme words ("What sound do you hear first in *cat*? in the middle of *cat*? At the end of *cat*?"). Examples of teaching these activities are provided in the fall and winter lessons in Chapter 4.

During weeks 16–19, the focus shifts to blending two and three phonemes together to come up with a word in the story just read aloud ("What word do we get if we blend these sounds together—/k/ /a/ /t/? Yes, *cat*"). Sample lessons are included in the winter and spring lessons in Chapter 4.

see it in Action

video
3

Hearing Beginning Sounds in Words

Four types of animals from *Mr. Gumpy's Outing* are printed on the chart. Nancy Sharp begins this part of the lesson by saying, "Now we are going to think about some of the animals in the story and we're going to listen for the beginning sound in the word. What was the first animal in the book?" Students respond with bunny rabbit. Nancy says, "The first sound in *rabbit* is /r/ abbit. What sound do you hear first, /r/?" Students say /r/. They move on to *cat* and then *dog*. Nancy has students slide their hand from the shoulder to the wrist of the opposite arm as they say the beginning sound, /d/ og. She asks, "What sound do you hear?" Some students call out *d*, but Nancy focuses them on the sound. "The first letter is *d*, but the sound is /d/."

tip

It's helpful if students say the beginning sound of the word with you as they start to slide their hand along their arm; it gets them actively involved. It's also a good idea if students once again tell you the beginning sound in the word, not just give you the letter name; it keeps them focused on phonemic awareness, an auditory ability. When students offer the letter name, coach for the sound as Nancy does.

ʃee it iN ActioN

Hearing Beginning and Ending Sounds in Words

After working on letter sounds from an alphabet book, Nancy Sharp moves on to hearing the beginning and ending sound in words with just two sounds. They are reading the book *Go, Dog. Go!* When they come to the word *up* Nancy pauses and says, "What sound do we hear at the beginning of *up*, /ə/?" Students say /ə/. "What do we hear at the end of *up*, /ə/ /p/?" A student shouts out the letter name, and Nancy says, "The letter is *p* but the sound you hear is /p/." As students say the words with Nancy to hear the sounds, they slide their hand from the shoulder to the wrists of the opposite arm. When they come to the word *in* Nancy has them focus on the ending sound, a newer skill for them than hearing the beginning sound. When they come to *up* again Nancy is very explicit. "So what is the beginning sound? The sound that you hear at the beginning of *up* is /ə/. What is the last sound you hear in *up*? The sound you hear last in *up* is /p/."

 tip

In this video, Nancy slides one hand from the shoulder to the wrist of her other arm as she goes from the beginning to the ending sound in a word. This makes the concept of first sound and last sound more concrete.

ʃee it iN ActioN

Blending Sounds into Words

In this spring lesson, Paula Berger asks her students to say the word formed by the sounds she articulates as she reads from *Just Grandpa and Me*. She begins by saying, "Who is ready for a challenge as we reread our book today? As I give you the sounds to a word, I want you to tell me the word." After she reads about Little Critter needing a new suit, she stops and says, /n/ /ē/ /d/, and students call out *need*. She has students slide their hand down their opposite arm from their shoulders to their elbows to their wrists as they say the beginning, middle, and ending sounds of need, /n/ /ē/ /d/, *need*. She repeats this exercise with the word *big* when she reads the next page, which is about going to a big department store. When she comes to the word *me*, she stops to ask, "How do you spell *me*?" Students quickly call out, *m e*. After reading the page about getting the new suit, she stops and says, /s/ /ü/ /t/, and students come up with *suit*. She praises, "I just can't stump you today!"

Phonics and Decoding

Recognizing Letter-Sound Correspondence

The EIR lessons include frequent but fast-paced reviews of letter names and letter sounds as students enjoy humorous alphabet books. Sixteen of the twenty-seven weekly lessons focus on multiple letters and their corresponding sounds. Some students will need little or no practice, but the ones who do can get more support from you during the small-group follow-up lessons.

see it iN ActioN

video 6

Learning Letter-Sound Correspondence

Nancy Sharp works on letter-sound correspondence and phonemic awareness as her students look for alphabet book pictures that begin with the letter *b*. "The letter *b* is the first letter we'll look at and the sound for *b* is /b/." Nancy reads, "Boris the bull waits for . . . ." She asks, "Can you see a blue butterfly? What words begin with /b/?" One boy offers, "Butterfly." Nancy coaches them to come up with *blue* as well. They look for pictures of words that begin with /b/ and find one of a bull. Nancy says, "Let's try it, slide your hand down your other arm as we say the word, /b/*ull*. Does it start with /b/? Yes it does." They move on to the sound /k/ for the letter *c*. They start with *cow*, sliding their hand down their arm as they say /k/*ow*. Next, one girl points to the spider on the page. Nancy says, "Let's try it—/s/*pider*, /k/*ow*. Is it the same or different?" The little girl says it is different.

 tip

It's hard to say the sounds in isolation of consonants that are stop sounds (*b, c, t*) rather than continuous sounds (*f, m, s*). Avoid a distinct and prolonged /uh/ at the end of the sound, as in /buh/, because it makes it difficult for students to hear the sound you are trying to say. Also, saying /buh/ a/ /tuh/ makes it hard for students to segment sounds into the word. In the video clip, Nancy says /b/ quickly several times to avoid saying a longer /buh/. This is one way to handle the issue. Another is to say the sound once, but quickly.

Interactive Sentence Writing

Listening carefully for the phonemes in words and then writing them down is important for students' phonemic awareness development and their emerging knowledge of sound-symbol correspondences. In interactive writing the teacher usually asks the children for ideas, then skillfully but quickly comes up with a sentence for the group to write. Often students come up with a sentence that is too long or difficult; in this case, their ideas need to be shortened and simplified into a similar but reasonable sentence.

Beginning in week 16, the children help the teacher come up with the sounds they hear in words in a sentence they are writing about a story. Later, the children each write the same sentence on their own, saying each word, listening for the sounds in sequence, and writing the letters that go with these sounds. The teacher can write the sentence as well, but should try to be a step behind the children so they don't simply copy. Instructional examples are provided in the winter and spring lessons in Chapter 4.

If children get stuck on a short vowel sound spelled with a single letter, don't just tell them the letter; teach them to use a short vowel chart (see Figure 3–4) to figure out how to spell a word with a particular short vowel sound. For example, help them figure out that the second sound in *bus* is the sound that is heard at the beginning of *umbrella*. Make sure the short vowel chart is available as you teach. Also, keep an alphabet card with both upper- and lowercase letters on each table in case a child forgets how to write a particular letter.

Since the purpose of writing sentences is to develop children's phonemic awareness, phonics knowledge, and reading ability, and since they will be rereading their sentences at school and perhaps at home, I recommend correct spelling. This is relatively easy to do when everyone is writing the sentence together. However, when children are writing on their own, they will probably use approximate spellings.

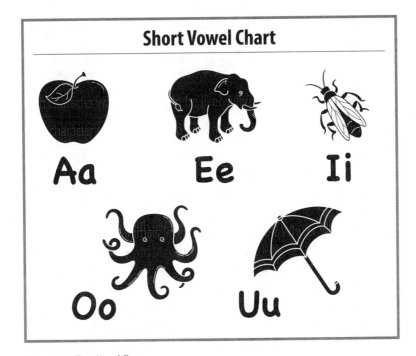

Figure 3–4 Short Vowel Chart

tip

Saying the word they are trying to write helps children focus on the phonemes. Write along with the children so they can check their work but try to stay a step behind so they don't simply try to copy. Your goal is for the children to be actively trying to hear the sounds in the words as they are writing them.

tip

Let children do as much as they can on their own and provide support as needed. Paula provides a good example of this here. The students were able to come up with the letters for the sounds in *he* and *went* and knew *to* and *the* on sight. They needed some help with the letters for some of the sounds in *store* and did not know that *store* had a silent *e* at the end.

See it in Action

video 7

Interactive Sentence Writing

Paula Berger works with her students on writing a sentence about their story *Just Grandpa and Me*. Each student has a whiteboard and marker. Paula begins, "Tell me a sentence about the story. Let's talk about where he was going." A student says, "He went to the store." Paula says, "Let's say *he*. How do we spell *he*, /h/ /ē/? Students call out *h e*. Paula writes *He* on the classroom whiteboard as students write the word on their own whiteboards. (They are writing on their own, not waiting to copy what Paula has written.) Paula moves on to *went*. "What does *went* start with, /w/? Students come up with *w*. Paula moves on to /e/, then /n/, and finally /t/. Students call out *e, n,* and *t* as Paula gets them to focus on the different sounds in the word. Students quickly spell *to* and *the,* because these are basic sight words on their word wall. Paula helps them with the *or* in *store* and tells them there is a silent *e* at the end of the word. She asks them to watch as she tracks the words while she rereads the sentence. She also asks them to hold up their whiteboards so she can take a quick look at how they have done.

tip

It is much more powerful if children write as you are writing rather than simply watch you write.

tip

In addition to developing her students' phonemic awareness and letter-sound knowledge, Paula also models tracking the words as they reread the sentence, another important emergent reading ability.

Sound Boxes

Begin this activity during week 19. As you say the sounds that make up two or three words from the story, have students point to and trace the letters you have written in the sound boxes (see the example in Figure 3–5). Then have them say the word they have traced. (Do this with each word at least twice.)

During week 20, have the children write the letter or letters for each sound, one sound per box, in two or three words from the story. After writing the words in boxes, children should touch the letters with their finger as they reread the words. This helps them make the transition from hearing the sounds in words and writing the letters for these sounds to reading the words. This activity helps children hear the sounds in words, develops their phonemic awareness, and helps them learn symbol-sound correspondence.

Sound Boxes for *Wild Bears* by Seymour Simon

1.	r	u	n	
2.	f	r	n	
3.	n	u	t	s

Figure 3–5 Sound Boxes for Wild Bears *by Seymour Simon*

As students become more adept, pull back on exaggerating the sounds for them (let them do this on their own if they need to). They are often more successful if they say the words themselves. Asking them how many sounds they hear in a word lets them know how many boxes to use. To help students become more independent, use a short vowel chart in which the vowels and pictures starting with each short vowel sound are displayed: *a—apple, e—elephant, i—insect, o—octopus, u—umbrella* (see Figure 3–4).

Concepts of Print and Decoding: Tracking Print

Accomplished kindergarten teachers frequently help their students track print while reading from a big book, chart, or individual books (Taylor et al. 2000). During weeks 22 and 23 support children as they track while they read with you (examples are included in the spring lessons in Chapter 4). Remember, this activity is done from the perspective of exposure, not mastery.

ʃee it iN ActioN

Tracking Print

Nancy Sharp and her students work on hearing and identifying the number of words in a sentence. They also talk about reading from left to right with a return sweep down to the next line of text "as readers need to do." Nancy begins, "Today we are going to talk about how many words there are in a sentence and how we can tell where each word is in a sentence." One boy ventures, "There are spaces." Nancy coaches him to elaborate, but he is unable to, so she does it for him, "There are spaces between the words." Nancy models, tracking the words as she reads aloud a sentence from the story that she has placed on a chart in front of the group: *I'd like a ride.* She has students read it again with her as they clap for each word and then tell her how many words there are in the sentence. Next, she has a student come up and track the words as she rereads the sentence. The tasks are not easy for these students, but they read through two more sentences from the story and are doing quite well by the end of the clip.

Comprehension Strategies: Summarizing Narrative and Informational Text by Engaging in Interactive Writing

In the winter and spring, you use interactive writing to teach students about summarizing narrative and informational texts. With narrative texts, you write one sentence a day that tells about the beginning (main character or characters and problem), middle (events, more on the problem), and end (resolution to the problem) of a story. You can talk about the author's message with a book such as *The Little Red Hen* (see week 21 in Chapter 4).

With informational books, you teach students about summarizing the big ideas. For example, for a book about what animals need to survive you can write two sentences together on two different days about main points in the book (see the lesson for week 22 in Chapter 4): *Animals need food, water, and safety. Baby animals need care.*

The EIR small-group lesson should be taught by a licensed teacher. Children who are having trouble learning to read need extra quality instruction from those who have the most expertise.

> ☑ **tip**

Daily Opportunity for Small-Group Practice

In addition to working with you daily as part of the whole group, students who are having difficulty with emergent literacy skills should also work on the whole-group activities again in a small-group follow-up lesson. Each sample weekly lesson in Chapter 4 includes examples of what should be covered in these practice sessions.

Professional Development

Each month, the new activities to be covered in the lessons for the following month are discussed in EIR professional learning sessions. Agendas for these monthly professional learning sessions are presented in Chapter 7. You may wish to review this section and the examples in Chapter 4 when you meet monthly with other teachers who are using the kindergarten program. In addition, you should discuss the lessons for the month just completed and children's successes and difficulties with these skills.

DISCUSS WITH YOUR COLLEAGUES

Discuss the idea of exposure, not mastery, which is an important underlying concept behind the EIR kindergarten program.

Discuss different ways in which you will be able to give the target children additional help with the activities covered in the whole-class weekly lesson. This instruction should be provided by a teacher, not an aide, since these children are at greatest risk of failing to learn to read in grade 1.

Weekly Lessons Introducing Key Emergent Literacy Skills

T he essential emergent literacy abilities discussed and summarized in Chapter 3 are taught in weekly whole-class lessons centered on two or more picture books. Each daily lesson should last no more than 10 or 15 minutes. (If you do not finish an activity on a given day, you can do so the next, but don't push back subsequent lessons; keeping to the schedule is essential so you get through all of the essential skills.) Also, each day you should spend about ten minutes repeating (or perhaps finishing) the whole-group activities with a small targeted group of struggling students who need more practice and support. Figures 4–1, 4–3, and 4–4 are summary charts capturing the scope and sequence of the lessons (these charts are also provided on the DVD). Example lessons for weeks marked with an asterisk, for skills taught for the first time, are presented in this chapter; example lessons for the remaining weeks are included on the accompanying DVD. Lesson planners to create your own lessons with books of your own choosing are also provided on the DVD.

Fall Lessons: September–December, Weeks 1–6

Week	New Activities	Repeat Activities	Exemplar Books
1*	**Discuss texts** **Explore vocabulary** **Act out text** **Explore concepts (body parts)**		*The 20th Century Children's Poetry Treasury*
	Identify letters A–L	Explore concepts (colors, feelings)	*Babar's ABC*
2		Explore concepts (colors, opposites, feelings)	*Go, Dog. Go!*
	Identify letters M–Z	Explore concepts	*Babar's ABC*
		Discuss text Explore vocabulary Explore concepts	*The 20th Century Children's Poetry Treasury*
3*	**Identify and produce rhyming words**	Discuss text Explore vocabulary	*The 20th Century Children's Poetry Treasury*
		Act out text Explore rhyme Explore concepts	*Over in the Meadow*
4*	**Identify (hear number of) words in a sentence** **Observe as teacher points to each word while reading a text summary** **Develop understanding that readers read left to right, with a return sweep to the next line**	Discuss texts	*The Little Panda*
		Identify letters A–Z	*Babar's ABC*
		Explore rhyme Discuss text Explore vocabulary	*The 20th Century Children's Poetry Treasury*
5		Act out text Discuss text Explore vocabulary Identify (hear number of) words in a sentence Explore concepts	*What Game Shall We Play?*
		Explore rhyme Discuss text Explore vocabulary	*The 20th Century Children's Poetry Treasury*
6*	**Hear and segment beginning sound in a word**	Act out text Discuss text Explore vocabulary Identify (hear number of) words in a sentence	*Mr. Gumpy's Outing*
	Identify pictures of things that begin with the sounds for A–H	Hear and segment the beginning sound in a word Identify letters A–H	*Usborne Farmyard Tales Alphabet Book*

Figure 4–1 *Fall Lessons: September–December, Weeks 1–11 (continues)*

Fall Lessons: September–December, Weeks 7–11

Week	New Activities	Repeat Activities	Exemplar Books
7		Act out text Discuss text Explore vocabulary Hear and segment beginning sound in a word	*Good-Night, Owl!*
	Identify pictures of things that begin with the sounds for I–R	Explore rhyme Hear and segment beginning sound in a word Identify letters I–R	*Usborne Farmyard Tales Alphabet Book*
8		Sing the text Act out the text Discuss the text Explore vocabulary Hear beginning sound in a word	*I Know an Old Lady*
	Identify pictures of things that begin with the sounds for S–Z	Hear and segment the beginning sound in a word Identify letters S–Z	*Usborne Farmyard Tales Alphabet Book*
9*	**Hear the beginning and ending sounds of a word**	Discuss text Explore vocabulary	*Signs on the Way*
	Identify and write upper- and lowercase A, B, C, D **Develop letter-sound correspondences A, B, C, D**	Identify pictures of things and words that begin with the sounds for A, B, C, D; identify the beginning and ending sound of a word.	*A, My Name Is Alice*
10*	**Hear and segment the ending sound in a word**	Act out text Discuss text Explore vocabulary	*The Three Billy Goats Gruff*
	Develop letter-sound correspondences E, F, G, H **Identify and write upper- and lowercase E, F, G, H**	Identify pictures of things and words that begin with the sounds for E, F, G, H. Hear the beginning and ending sound in a word	*A, My Name Is Alice*
11*	**Segment the sounds in words with two phonemes**	Act out text Discuss text	*Hattie and the Fox*
	Identify and write upper- and lowercase I, J, K, L **Develop letter-sound correspondence: I, J, K, L**	Identify pictures of things and words that begin with the sounds for I, J ,K, L Hear beginning and ending sound in a word	*A, My Name Is Alice*

*Lesson example provided in this chapter. Example lessons for the other weeks are on the DVD. Lesson planners for all weeks to use with your own books are also on the DVD.

Figure 4–1 Fall Lessons: September–December, Weeks 1–11 (continued)

Week 1
Book: *The 20th Century Children's Poetry Treasury*

New Activities: *Discuss text; explore vocabulary; explore concepts; act out text*

Select ten or so poems to read over the course of the week. Read some poems just for fun. Discuss some poems briefly, explore concepts and vocabulary when it is beneficial to students, and let students act out poems that lend themselves to doing so. Read each poem two or three times during the week. Examples:

Read "Tickle, Tickle" (p. 21) just for fun. Discuss what *prove* means. Then talk about the fact that the boy feels happy. If useful for some children, point out body parts as you read and talk about the poem.

Explore concepts: "How does the boy *feel*? How do we know? We look at his *face* [point it out] and see he's smiling. His *mouth* shows that he is smiling. His face is on his *head*. His *hands* are on his *arms* [point them out]. His *fingers* are on his hands [point them out]. Can you look like the boy?"

Discuss the poem: "Tell about something fun you like to do with someone in your family. What do you do together? Why do you like this? How do you feel? Share ideas with a partner." Let one or two students share their ideas.

Read "A Circle of Sun" (p. 4) twice, having children act it out the second time.

Additional Book for Week 1: *Babar's ABC*

New Activity: *Identify letters A–L*

Repeat Activities: *Discuss text and explore concepts*

Explore each letter two or three times during the week:

A: "What letter do we see on this page? What color is the letter *A*? Yes, white. The *A* is white. The letter *A* can make the sound /a/ or /ā/. What things do we see beginning with *A*?" Students will likely need help, so point out the arrow, apple, and accordion. "Why do you think the elephant is happy?"

B: "What letter do we see on this page? What color is the letter *B*? Yes, the letter *B* is yellow. The sound for letter *B* is /b/. What animals do we see that begin with the letter *B*?" [bear, bird]

Continue with letters C–K.

L: "What letter do we see on this page? What color is the letter *L*? Yes, the letter *L* is brown. The sound for letter *L* is /l/. What animals do we see that begin with the letter *L*? How do you think the lamb feels? Why?"

For children who need extra help: Each day reread some of the poems and explore some of the letters. Ask some of the same questions and talk about vocabulary from the book that you covered in the whole-group lesson so these children get another chance to respond.

New Activity: *Identify and produce rhyming words*

Repeat Activities: *Discuss text; explore vocabulary*

Each day reread one or two favorite poems from weeks 1 and 2. Talk with the children about the words that rhyme in each poem you reread. Also read one or two new poems every day. Get children to say the words that rhyme with you. Ask them to come up with more words that rhyme with each pair of rhyming words. Nonsense words are fine. Examples:

Read "Notice" (p. 50).

Discuss the poem: "What do you know about frogs? What would you like to learn? Maybe we can find out. What would you do if you had a frog inside your hat?"

Explore rhyme: "*Dog* and *frog* rhyme. They sound the same at the end, /og/ – /d/ /og/, /fr/ /og/. What are two other words that rhyme? What else rhymes with *cat* and *hat*? With *dog* and *frog*?"

Read "Concerning Love" (p. 51).

Discuss the poem: "Who has a cat? Another pet? Tell a partner about your pet if you have one or about a pet you would like to have. What do you do to take care of your pet? What do you like about your pet?"

Explore rhyme: "One word in the poem is *wish*. Who can think of a word that rhymes with *wish*?" Remember, nonsense words are fine at this point.

Additional Book for Week 3:
Over in the Meadow

Repeat Activities: *Explore rhyme; act out text; explore concepts*

Read through the book just for fun. On the second reading have the children do the motions that the animals are doing. Have them count the number of little animals on subsequent readings. Also, as you reread the book, get the children to say with you the words that rhyme on each page. Have them give you additional words that rhyme with these words. (Nonsense words are fine.) In addition, if useful to some children, discuss the following concepts:

Turtle (p. 1)	The mother is *big*. The child is *little*.
Fish (p. 2)	The dragonfly is *purple*. It is *over* or *above* the fish. The fish are *under* the dragonfly.
Birds (p. 3)	The birds are *blue*. The mother is *on* the branch. The little birds are *in* the tree. They look the *same*.
Muskrat (p. 4)	The muskrats are *brown*. The mother is *out* of the water. The children are diving *into* the water.

Bees (p. 5)	Four little bees look the *same* (they are *orange* and *black*), one looks *different* (*yellow* and *black*).
Crows (p. 6)	The little birds are *in* the nest.
Lizards (p. 8)	The mother is *on top of* the gate.
Frogs (p. 9)	The lily pad is *under* the little frogs. Some frogs are jumping *up.* Some are diving *down* into the water.
Firefly (p. 10)	The fireflies are *green.*

For children who need extra help: Each day reread some of the poems and talk about rhyming words. Ask some of the same questions and talk about vocabulary that you covered in the whole-group lesson so these children get a chance to respond again. Also repeat the activities you did with the large group as you reread *Over in the Meadow.*

New Activities: *Identify (hear number of) words in a sentence;* observe as teacher points to each word while reading a story summary; develop understanding that readers read left to right, with a return sweep to the next line.

Repeat Activities: *Discuss text; explore vocabulary*

Read the first time just for fun. As you read, briefly talk about the meanings of useful but unfamiliar words like *panda* and *forest*.

Discussion: "What do you like about this book? Why did you pick this part? Share with a partner." Have one or two students share their ideas. "What did we learn?"

Identifying the number of words: Have children clap for each word you read on three or four pages of the book. Start with page 4, which has just four words in the sentence. Point to each word with your finger as the children clap. (Show them there are four words on the line.) On page 8, also point out that when we read, we go across and down. (If you are using a different book, avoid clapping out sentences with multisyllabic words. This will be covered later.)

Additional Book for Week 4: *Babar's ABC*

Repeat Activity: *Identify letters A–Z*

Reread, asking the children to identify the letters and animals and other objects that begin with the sounds of these letters on each page.

Additional Book for Week 4: *The 20th Century Children's Poetry Treasury*

Repeat Activities: *Explore rhymes, explore vocabulary, discuss text, act out text*

Select 5–10 poems to read during the week. Ask students to identify rhymes after you read each poem. Have students share answers to questions with a partner, and then have one or two students share their ideas. For example:

"The Gentle Cow" (p. 8): *Vocabulary*: "What does *gentle* mean?" Tell students if they do not know.

"Tent" (p. 9): "What is a tent?"

"Night Sounds" (p. 14): *Vocabulary*: "What does *mumbling* mean? *grumbling*?" Tell students if no one knows. *Discussion*: "What sounds keep you from sleeping? What do you do about it? What sounds help you to sleep?"

"Big Sister" (p. 20): *Discussion*: "Do you like your [Would you like to have a] big brother or sister? Why? If you have a big brother or sister, how are you like them or how are you different?"

"Loose and Limber" (p. 34): *Vocabulary, acting out*: "Let's all be loose and limber." Show students how.

"Building a Skyscraper" (p. 54): *Vocabulary*: Point out the beams in the picture. "What does 'crowds of people stand and stare' mean?"

"Sneeze" (p. 76): "Who can show us a sneeze?"

For children who need extra help: Each day reread part of the story and have students identify the number of words in phrases or sentences. Ask some of the same questions and talk about vocabulary that you covered in the whole-group lesson and identify rhyming words so these children get a chance to respond and practice.

New Activity: *Hear and segment the beginning sound in a word*

Repeat Activities: *Act out text; discuss text; explore vocabulary; identify the number of words in a sentence*

Read the story just for fun the first time. Read a second time and have children *act it out*. As you read, briefly talk about the meaning of useful but unfamiliar words such as *squabble, trample, bank, field*. Next day, switch roles and act it out again. (Everyone can act out the page that starts "For a little while . . . .") On a subsequent rereading, focus on the following:

> *Discussion*: "Have you ever been to a party? What did you like about it? Was there a part you didn't like? Share with a partner."

> *Cat page*: As you track print, have children clap to identify the number of words in "I'd like a ride." Reread, track print, and count. Read, "Said the cat." Reread, track print, and count.

> *Dog page*: Have children clap to identify the number of words in, "Will you take me with you?" Reread, track print, and count. Read, "But don't tease the cat." Reread, track print, and count. Reread the whole page while tracking print; talk about how readers go from left to right, with a return sweep down to the next line.

On another subsequent rereading, focus on hearing and segmenting the beginning sound in a word. Being able to hear the phonemes or sounds in words is highly predictive of reading ability in first grade. For example:

> *Cat page*: "Let's listen carefully to the word *cat* — /k/ /k/ *cat*. It starts with the sound /k/ — *cat*, /k/, *cat*. This is something important that readers need to be able to hear. What do you hear at the beginning of *cat*? Yes, /k/ — *cat*."

> Go through the same procedure with *dog, pig,* and *goat*. You are not trying to teach the children the letter that goes with the sound. You are trying to develop their phonemic awareness.

Additional Book for Week 6:
Usborne Farmyard Tales and Alphabet Book

New Activity: *Identify pictures that begin with the sounds for A–H*

Repeat Activity: *Hear and segment the beginning sound in a word; identify letters A–H*

Read pages A–H with the students. Have students identify the letter on each page. Also look at all the things in the illustrations on each page that begin with this sound. "The sound of the letter *b* is /b/. On this page we see a barn. Barn starts with /b/, the sound of the letter *b*. Good readers need to know the sounds that letters make. What else can we find on this page that starts with /b/, the sound that the letter *b* makes?"

For children who need extra help: Each day, reread pages of the story you read with the whole group and have children identify the beginning sounds of words from the story. Also ask questions about the story that you asked in the whole-group lesson, such as (for *Mr. Gumpy's Outing*), "Have you ever been to a party? What did you like about it? Was there a part you didn't like?" Talk about vocabulary again. Also, identify pictures in the alphabet book that begin with the sounds for letters A–H.

Week 9
Book: *Signs on the Way*

New Activity: *Hear the beginning and ending sounds in a word*

Repeat Activities: *Discuss text; explore vocabulary*

First read the story just for fun. As you read, briefly talk about the meaning of useful but unfamiliar words, such as *speed limit* and *roadwork*.

Discussion: "What other signs do you know? Where do you see it? What does it mean? Share with a partner." Let a few students share their examples. "Why do we need signs?" Discuss.

Hearing the beginning and ending sounds in a word: On subsequent readings focus this new skill in phonemic awareness development. For example:

> Page 3: "Let's listen carefully to the sound you hear at the beginning of fast—/f/*ast*. What sound do you hear at the beginning of *fast*? Now, let's listen again. What sound do you hear at the end of *fast*? Fas/t/, *fast*."

> Repeat with several other one-syllable words from the story: *can, stop, we, us*.

Additional Book for Week 9: *A, My Name Is Alice*

New Activities: *Identify and write (or trace) lower- and uppercase A, B, C, D; develop letter-sound correspondence* for A, B, C, D

Repeat Activities: *Identify pictures that begin with a particular sound; identify the sound they hear at the beginning and end of a word*

Read pages A–D. Work on identifying and writing (or tracing) lower- and uppercase letters. Keep in mind that the objective is exposure, not mastery. Point out the upper- and lowercase version of each letter in the words on the chart in Figure 4–2 (and on the DVD). Give children a copy of this chart, and have them write (or trace) the *A* in *Alice*, the *A* in *Alex*, and the *a* in *ants*. Tell students the sound that each beginning letter makes as you say the word: "The *A* in *Alice* sounds like /a/." Have them repeat the sound. "Alice is an ape. The letter *a* in *ape* sounds like /ā/." Have them repeat each word after you say it. Also work on identifying words that begin with a particular sound (again, the objective is exposure, not mastery):

> A: Have them identify pictures of things that begin with a particular sound such as the /a/ or /ā/ sound (*ant, ape*).

> B: Have them identify pictures of things that begin with the /b/ sound.

> C: Have them identify pictures of things that begin with hard *c*, /k/.

> D: Have them identify pictures of things that begin with /d/. Ask what they hear at the beginning of *duck*. What do they hear at the end of *duck*? *Dust*?

Alice	Alex	ants
Barbara	Bob	balloons
Clara	Claude	cakes
Doris	Dave	dust

Figure 4–2 Chart for Week 9 Lesson

For children who need extra help: Each day reread part of the story and help students hear the beginning and ending sounds in a word. Ask some of the same questions and talk about vocabulary that you covered in the whole-group lesson. Using the alphabet book, work on identifying and writing (or tracing) lower- and uppercase letters and developing the letter-sound correspondences for A, B, C, and D. Work again on identifying pictures of things or words on each page that begin with A, B, C, and D. With the informational book, work on hearing the beginning and ending sound in some of the words you covered in the whole-group lesson.

New Activity: *Hear and segment the ending sound of a word*

Repeat Activities: *Act out text; discuss text; explore vocabulary*

Read the story the first time just for fun. As you read, briefly talk about the meaning of useful but unfamiliar words: *valley, meadow, hooves, rushing river.* Form two groups of four students and have them act out the story as you reread it. Next time, let other groups act it out.

Discussion: "The troll is a bully. What is a bully? What can you do if someone is being a bully?"

Identifying the ending sound: Have them identify the ending sound in *gruff, troll, trip, trap, snip, snap, snout.* "What sound do you hear at the end of *gruff*? *Gru*/f/. Yes, the ending sound is /f/."

Additional Book for Week 10: *A, My Name Is Alice*

New Activities: *Identify and write (or trace) lower- and uppercase E, F, G, H; develop symbol-sound correspondences for E, F, G, H*

Repeat Activities: *Identify pictures and words on each page that begin with the sounds for E, F, G, H; hear beginning and ending sounds in a word*

Read pages E–H. Point out the upper- and lowercase version of each letter in the words on a chart you've prepared (give each student a copy). Have the children *write (or trace) each letter* at the beginning of these words. Let those who are able write each letter. Tell students the sound that each beginning letter makes as you say a word that begins with the letter you are focusing on. Have them repeat the sound. Have them repeat each word after you say it to help them develop letter-sound correspondences. Also work on identifying pictures of things or words on each page that begin with the sounds for E, F, G, and H. Remember, the objective is exposure, not mastery.

For children who need extra help: Each day, reread part of the story and help students identify the ending sound in a word. Ask some of the same questions and talk about vocabulary that you covered in the whole-group lesson. Using the alphabet book, work on developing letter-sound correspondences for E, F, G, H and identifying and writing these letters.

Week 11
Book: *Hattie and the Fox*

New Activity: *Segment the sounds in words with two phonemes (consonant-vowel or vowel-consonant)*

Repeat Activities: *Act out text; discuss text*

Read the story first just for fun. Then assign parts and have the children act it out. On subsequent rereadings, have different children act it out or have them all chime in on the refrain.

Discussion: "Think about a time you've been afraid of something. What made you afraid? What did you do about it? Share with a partner."

Segmenting sounds in words with two phonemes (consonant-vowel or vowel-consonant):

Page 1: Repeat "Goodness gracious me." Ask the children to give you the sound they hear first in *me*, /m/, and the sound they hear next, /ē/.

Page 3: Repeat "'So what?' said the horse." Ask the children to give you the sound they hear first in *so*, /s/, and the sound they hear next, /ō/.

Page 4: Repeat "I can see a nose and two eyes in the bushes." Ask the children to give you the sound they hear first in *see*, /s/, and the sound they hear next, /ē/.

Page 5: Repeat "But the cow said, 'Moo.'" Ask the children to give you the sound they hear first in *moo*, /m/ and the sound they hear next, /ü/.

Additional Book for Week 11: *A, My Name Is Alice*

New Activities: *Identify and write (or trace) lower- and uppercase letters I, J, K, L; develop letter-sound correspondences for I, J, K, L*

Repeat Activities: *Identify pictures and words on each page that begin with the sounds for I, J, K, L; hear the beginning and ending sounds in a word*

Read pages I–L. Point out the upper- and lowercase version of each letter of the words on a chart you have prepared (give each student a copy). Have the children write (or trace) each letter at the beginning of each word. Let those who are able to write each letter do so. Tell students the sound that each beginning letter makes as you say the word that begins with the letter you are focusing on. Have them repeat the sound. Have them repeat each word after you say it to help them develop letter-sound correspondences. Also work on identifying pictures and words on each page that begin with the sound of that letter. Remember, the objective is exposure, not mastery.

Hearing the beginning and ending sounds in a word:

I : Ask what they hear at the beginning of *Ida* and the end of *Ida*. Repeat with *Ivan*.

J: Ask what they hear at the beginning of *Jane* and the end of *Jane*. Repeat with *John*.

K: Ask what they hear at the beginning of *kiss* and the end of *kiss*.

L: Ask what they hear at the beginning of *Luke* and the end of *Luke*. Repeat with *loon*.

For children who need extra help: Each day reread part of the story and work with students on segmenting all the sounds in words with two phonemes (consonant-vowel or vowel-consonant). Ask some of the same questions and talk about vocabulary that you covered in the whole-group lesson. Using the alphabet book, work on developing letter-sound correspondences for I, J, K, L and identifying and writing these letters. Work with students on hearing the beginning and ending sound in a word.

Winter Lessons: January–February, Weeks 12–15

Week	New Activities	Repeat Activities	Exemplar Books
12		Act out text Discuss text Explore vocabulary Segment the sounds in words with two phonemes	*Are You My Mother?*
	Identify and write upper- and lowercase M, N, O, P Develop letter-sound correspondences M, N, O, P	Identify pictures of things and words that begin with the sounds for M, N, O, P Hear beginning and ending sounds in words	*A, My Name Is Alice*
		Sing Act out story	*Peanut Butter and Jelly*
13*	**Segment the sounds in three-phoneme words**	Discuss story Explore vocabulary	*Do Like Kyla*
	Identify and write upper- and lowercase Q, R, S, T Develop letter-sound correspondences Q[U], R, S, T	Identify pictures of things and words that begin with the sounds for Q, R, S, T Hear beginning and ending sounds in words	*A, My Name Is Alice*
		Explore rhyme	*The 20th Century Children's Poetry Treasury*
14		Act out story Discuss story Explore vocabulary Segment the sounds in three-phoneme words	*The Mitten*
	Identify and write upper- and lowercase U, V, W, X, Y, Z Develop letter-sound correspondences U, V, W, X, Y, Z	Identify pictures of things and words that begin with the sounds for U, V, W, X, Y, Z Hear beginning and ending sounds in words	*A, My Name Is Alice*
		Explore rhyme	*The 20th Century Children's Poetry Treasury*
15		Discuss story Explore vocabulary Segment sounds in three-phoneme words	*Time to Sleep*
		Identify letters A–Z Give the sounds for the consonants Write upper- and lowercase letters	*Babar's ABC*

Figure 4–3 Winter Lessons: January–February, Weeks 12–18 (continues)

Winter Lessons: January–February, Weeks 16–18

Week	New Activities	Repeat Activities	Exemplar Books
16*	Engage in interactive sentence writing	Act out story Discuss story	*Jump, Frog, Jump!*
	Blend two phonemes to make a word in an oral sentence		*Go Dog. Go!*
17*	Say words by blending three phonemes of the word pronounced by teacher Summarize a narrative text by engaging in interactive sentence writing	Discuss story Explore vocabulary	*Whistle for Willie*
		Discuss story Learn vocabulary Say words by blending three phonemes pronounced by teacher	*A Bird Flies By*
		Identify beginning sounds in words Write upper- and lowercase letters Identify letters A–M Give the sounds for the letters A, B, C, D, F, G, H, J, K, L, M	*Usborne Farmyard Tales Alphabet Book*
18*	Say three-letter words from the story by blending phonemes pronounced by teacher in isolation after reading the story	Act out story Discuss story Explore vocabulary Say words by blending three phonemes you pronounce Write a sentence interactively	*Good Morning, Chick*
		Identify beginning sounds in words Write upper- and lowercase letters N–Z Identify letters N–Z Give the sounds for the letters N, O, P, Q[U], R, S, T, U, V, W, Y, Z	*Usborne Farmyard Tales Alphabet Book*

*Lesson example provided in this chapter. Example lessons for the other weeks are on the DVD. Lesson planners for all weeks to use with your own books are also on the DVD.

Figure 4–3 Winter Lessons: January–February, Weeks 12–18 (continued)

Week 13
Book: *Do Like Kyla*

New Activity: *Segment the sounds in three-phoneme words*

Repeat Activities: *Discuss text; explore vocabulary*

First read the story just for fun. Then reread it, focusing on segmenting the sounds in three-phoneme words. As you read, briefly talk about the meaning of useful but unfamiliar words such as *quick fingers, honey, sunbeam.*

Discussion: "Do you have an older brother, sister, cousin, or neighbor you like to do things with? What things do you do and why do you like to do things with this person? Share your ideas with your partner."

Segmenting sounds in three-phoneme words: Reread the sentence that contains each of the words below and segment the sounds in the words:

Page 1:   "The first sound you hear in *bed* is /b/, the next sound you hear in *bed* is /e/, and the end sound you hear in bed is /d/. *Bed.* /B/ /e/ /d/." Have students say the sounds in the words with you. It often helps if students slide their hand from the shoulder to the elbow to the wrist of their opposite arm as they say the beginning, middle, and end sound in the word.

Page 2:   *Head, like*

Page 3:   *Sit, big*

Page 7:   *Kiss, head*

Page 9:   *Got*

Page 10:   *Big*

Page 11:   *Bag, jam*

Page 14:   *Page*

Page 15:   *Tap*

Additional Book for Week 13: *A, My Name Is Alice*

New Activities: *Identify and write (or trace) lower- and uppercase letters; develop letter-sound correspondences for Q[U], R, S, T*

Repeat Activities: *Identify pictures and words that begin with the sound for Q, R, S, T; hear the beginning and ending sounds in a word*

Read pages Q–T. Point out the upper- and lowercase version of each letter on a chart. Have the children write (or trace) each letter. Let those who are able write each letter. Have the children repeat each word after you say it to emphasize letter-sound correspondence. Have them identify pictures or words on each page that begin with the sounds for Q[U], R, S, T. Also, work with students on hearing the beginning and ending sound in a word:

R: "What do you hear at the beginning and end of *rat*?"

T: "What do you hear at the beginning and end of *Ted*? *Tiger*?"

Additional Book for Week 13:
The 20th Century Children's Poetry Treasury

Repeat Activity: *Explore rhyme*

Reread favorite poems. Identify and talk about the words that rhyme.

For children who need extra help: Each day reread part of the story and work on segmenting all the sounds in words with three phonemes. Ask some of the same questions and talk about vocabulary that you covered in the whole-group lesson. Using the alphabet book, work on developing letter-sound correspondences for Q[U], R, S, T and identifying and writing these letters. Work with students on hearing the beginning and ending sound in a word.

Week 16
Book: *Jump, Frog, Jump!*

New Activity: *Interactive sentence writing*

Repeat Activities: *Discuss text; act out text*

Read the story first for fun. On subsequent rereadings have the children *act it out*.

Discussion: "Has a pet ever gotten away from you when you were trying to catch it? How did you feel? What did you do? Have you ever caught a bug and then let it go? Have you ever tried to catch a bug but couldn't do it? Tell a partner about it." Let a few children share briefly.

Interactive Sentence Writing: On two days during the week have the group generate a sentence about the story (a different sentence each day). Have them watch and help as you write each sentence on a chart. Example: *The frog jumped away*. Ask how many words they hear in the sentence. Write *The*. Talk about starting on the left and going right. Talk about starting with a capital *T*. "What do you hear at the beginning of *frog*? Yes, /f/. What else do you hear? Okay, /g/ is at the end. In the middle we have /r/ and /o/—/f/ /r/ /o/ /g/, *frog*." Write *frog*. "What do you hear at the beginning of *jumped*? Yes, /j/." Write *j*. "What else do you hear? You hear an /m/. Great. And before the /m/ there is a letter *u* for /ə/." Show them the short vowel chart (Figure 3–4 in Chapter 3) and tell them the /ə/ in *jump* is just like the sound for *u* in *umbrella*. Write *u m*. Ask what else they hear. Exaggerate the *p* if necessary. "Yes, /p/." Write the *p*. Tell them the word ends with *ed*. Write *away* for them. Have them reread the sentence with you as you point to each word. "I'm going to leave our sentence on the chart, and you can come up sometime during the day to read it again to yourself or with a partner."

Additional Book for Week 16: *Go Dog. Go!*

New Activity: *Blend two phonemes to make a word in an oral sentence*

Read the book just for fun. Then work on the new skill of blending two phonemes (sounds) together into a word:

Page 10: After reading the page say, "If I put these two sounds together, /i/ /n/, what word do I get? Yes, *in*. /i/ /n/, *in*."

Page 16: "I want to see if you can tell me the last word on this page if I give you the sounds: / ə/ /p/. Yes, *up*."

Page 18: ". . . /i/ /z/. Yes, *is*."

Page 26: ". . . /m/ /y/. Yes, *my*."

Pages 27–28: /G/ /o/

Page 31: /i/ /t/

Page 33: /a/ /t/

For children who need extra help: Each day reread part of *Jump, Frog, Jump!*
and write a sentence about the story interactively (the same one you used with
the whole group or a different one). Ask some of the same questions that you
asked about the story in the whole-group lesson. Using *Go, Dog. Go!* work on
blending two sounds to come up with a two-phoneme word in a sentence.

Week 17
Book: *Whistle for Willie*

New Activities: *Say words by blending three phonemes pronounced by the teacher; summarize a narrative text by engaging in interactive sentence writing.*

Repeat Activities: *Discuss text; explore vocabulary*

Read the story just for fun. As you read, briefly talk about the meaning of useful but unfamiliar words, such as *pretend, scrambled, errand*.

Discussion: "Can you whistle? Try it. How did you learn? What is something you just learned how to do? How did you feel? Tell a partner about it."

Blending three phonemes into a word: As you reread the story, stop to give the sounds for three-phoneme words. For example:

Page 2:   "'He saw a boy playing with his /d/ /o/ /g/.' Yes, *dog*. 'Whenever the boy whistled, the dog /r/ /a/ /n/'—yes, *ran*—'straight to /h/ /i/ /m/.' Yes, *him*."

Page 6:   *His, hid*

Page 8:   *Got, home, line*

Page 10:   *Hat, feel*

Page 13:   *Run*

Page 19:   *Ran, did*

New Activity: *Summarize a narrative by writing a sentence interactively*

Interactively, write three sentences (one a day for three days) that summarize the book. Have the children give you as many of the sounds in the words and letters to those sounds as they can. Write the sentences on a chart and leave it where children can reread the sentences if they wish.

Day 1: Ask what happened at the beginning of the story. Lead students to a sentence that includes the main character and problem—*Peter can not whistle*, for example. Ask students for the sounds in the first three words. When you come to the *a* in *can* and the *o* in *not*, use the short vowel chart to help them remember the short vowel sounds for *a* as in *apple* and *o* as in *octopus*. Tell them as you write that there is a silent *e* before the *r* in *Peter*. Write *whistle* for them.

Day 2: Ask what happened in the middle of the story related to Peter's problem. Lead them to a sentence such as, *Peter keeps trying to whistle*. Have students help you with as many of the sounds in the words as they can.

Day 3: Ask what happened at the end of the story and how the problem got solved. Lead students to a sentence such as, *Then Peter whistles at his dog*.

Additional Book for Week 17: *A Bird Flies By*

Repeat Activities: *Blend two phonemes into words; discuss text*

Read the book just for fun. Stop to talk about the birds in the pictures.

Discussion: "What did you learn about birds? What else would you like to learn? Maybe we can find out more. Share your ideas with your partner about it. What birds do you see? Where do you see them? What do you like about birds? Share with a partner." Let a few students share their ideas for each question with the whole group.

Blending two phonemes into a word: "I'm going to stop and give the sounds for a few words from the story. See if you can tell me each word as I stop reading the sentence." Reread the following pages, stopping at the words indicated:

Page 2:   /b/ /y/, *by*

Page 4:   /i/ /z/, *is*

Page 6:   /i/ /n/, *in*

Page 8:   /i/ /t/, *it*

Page 12:   /s/ /ē/, *sea*

Additional Book for Week 17: *Usborne Farmyard Tales Alphabet Book*

Repeat Activities: *Identify beginning sounds, identify and write upper- and lower-case letters; identify letters A–N; give sounds for letters A–N*

Read A–N. Have students identify the beginning sound in *apple, bull, cows, doll, egg, fish, hens, insect/ice cream, jet, kittens, mice, nest*. Have them identify and write the upper- and lowercase letters. Have them give the sounds that letters A–N make.

For children who need extra help: Each day reread part of the story and work on blending three phonemes into a word, just as you did in the whole-group lesson. Also write a sentence interactively about *Whistle for Willie* (the same sentence you used in the large group or a different one). Ask some of the same questions and talk about vocabulary that you covered in the whole-group lesson. Using *A Bird Flies By*, work on blending two sounds to come up with the words from the story, just as you did during the large-group lesson.

New Activity: *Say three-letter words from the story by blending phonemes pronounced by the teacher in isolation after reading the story.*

Repeat Activities: *Act out text; discuss text; explore vocabulary; blend three phonemes within a sentence to generate a word; write a sentence interactively*

First read the book just for fun. As you read, briefly talk about the meaning of useful but unfamiliar words, such as *smooth, fluffy, beak, rooster*. Reread the story several times and have various children act it out.

Discussion: "What is something you'd like to be able to do that you can't do yet? How will you try to learn this? Share with a partner." Let a few children share their ideas.

Blending the sounds for three-phoneme words into the correct word: As you reread the story, stop and give the sounds for a few words, have students blend the sounds and give you the word, and continue reading the sentence:

Page 2: /t/ /a/ /p/, *tap*

Page 3: /k/ /ā/ /m/, *came*

Page 4: /b/ /ē/ /k/, *beak*; /f/ /ē/ /t/, *feet*

Page 5: /n/ /ā/ /m/, *name*; /h/ /e/ /n/, *hen*

Page 6: /p/ /e/ /k/, *peck*

Page 7: /k/ /a/ /t/, *cat*

Page 9: /n/ /e/ /k/, *neck*

Page 10: /r/ /a/ /n/, *ran*

Page 11: /f/ /e/ /l/, *fell*

Page 12: /k/ /a/ /n/, *can*

Finish the story.

New Activity: *Blending three phonemes into a word in isolation (not in a sentence)*

"Now, I'm going to say some words from the story and you see if you can tell me what they are." [/t/ /a/ /p/, *tap*; /b/ /ē/ /k/, *beak*; /h/ /e/ /n/, *hen*; /p/ /e/ /k/, *peck*; /r/ /a/ /n/, *ran*]

Interactive writing: On each of two days write a different group sentence about the story. Have children give you as many of the sounds in the words and letters for those sounds as they can. Remember to use the short vowel chart for short vowel sounds. If children are able, have them try to write one of the sentences (keep it very short) on their own paper as you write on the chart.

Additional Book:
Usborne Farmyard Tales Alphabet Book

Repeat Activities: *Identify beginning sounds in words; write upper- and lowercase letters N–Z; identify letters N–Z; give the sounds for the letters N–Z*

Reread pages O–Z. Have students identify the beginning sounds in *ostrich, pony, rabbits, turkeys, umbrella, van, zebra.* Have them identify and write the upper- and lowercase letters. Have them give the sounds that letters N–Z make.

For children who need extra help: Each day reread part of *Good Morning, Chick* and work on blending three phonemes into a word, just as you did in the whole-group lesson. Also write a sentence interactively about *Good Morning, Chick* (the same sentence you used in the large-group or a different one). Ask some of the same questions and talk about vocabulary that you covered in the whole-group lesson. Using *Usborne Farmyard Tales Alphabet Book,* work on identifying beginning sounds in words, writing upper- and lowercase letters N–Z, identifying letters N–Z, and generating letter-sound correspondences for N, O, P, Q[U], R, S, T, U, V, W, X, Y, Z.

Spring Lessons: March–May, Weeks 19–22

Week	New Activities	Repeat Activities	Exemplar Books
19*	**Point to, say, and blend three letters (in sound boxes) that represent the phonemes of a word**	Act out text Discuss text Explore vocabulary Summarize a narrative by writing a sentence interactively	*Jamaica Tag-Along*
20*	**Write letters of three-phoneme words in sound boxes**	Discuss text Explore vocabulary Say three-phoneme words from the story (in isolation) by blending phonemes you pronounce Segment beginning, middle, and ending sounds in a three-phoneme word Write a sentence interactively	*Jamaica and Briana*
		Discuss text Explore vocabulary Say three-phoneme words from the story (in isolation) by blending phonemes they have heard you pronounce	*Just Grandpa and Me*
21*	**Hear the two parts in two-syllable words**	Act out text Discuss text Explore vocabulary Summarize a narrative by writing a sentence interactively Observe teacher pointing to each word while reading a story summary Recognize that readers read left to right, with a return sweep to the next line	*The Little Red Hen*
	Summarize informational text by writing a sentence interactively	Discuss text Explore vocabulary Write three-phoneme words in sound boxes Blend three phonemes in sound boxes to read words in isolation	*Wild Bears*
22*	**Track print while reading, pointing to each word as it is read and not confusing two-syllable words for two words**	Discuss text Explore vocabulary Recognize directionality used in reading (left to right, down, and to the left) Segment beginning, middle, and end sounds in two- and three-phoneme words and write sounds in sound boxes Blend three phonemes in sound boxes to read words in isolation	*Ant*
		Discuss text Summarize informational text by writing a sentence interactively	*What Animals Need*
		Identify upper- and lowercase letters A–H Give sounds for letters A–H	*A, My Name Is Alice*

Figure 4–4 Spring Lessons: March–May, Weeks 19–27 (continues)

Spring Lessons: March–May, Weeks 22–25

Week	New Activities	Repeat Activities	Exemplar Books
22*		Explore rhyme Act out text	*The 20th Century Children's Poetry Treasury*
23		Discuss text Explore vocabulary Segment sounds in a three-phoneme word and write sounds in sound boxes Track print while reading Write a sentence interactively	*Ant*
		Identify upper- and lowercase letters I–P Give sounds for letters I–P	*A, My Name Is Alice*
		Explore rhyme Act out text	*The 20th Century Children's Poetry Treasury*
		Select a favorite story from earlier in the year to act out	*Favorite story*
24		Discuss text Explore vocabulary Segment sounds in a three-phoneme word and write letters for these sounds in sound boxes Track print while reading Write a sentence interactively	*Ant*
		Identify upper- and lowercase letters Q–Z Give sounds for letters Q[U]–Z	*A, My Name Is Alice*
		Explore rhyme Act out text	*The 20th Century Children's Poetry Treasury*
		Select a favorite story from earlier in the year to act out	*Favorite story*
25*	**For a C-V-C word from the story, write more words that belong to same word family**	Discuss text Explore vocabulary Write a sentence interactively	*Caterpillar*
		Identify, give sounds for lower- and uppercase letters A–H	*Babar's ABC*
		Explore rhyme	*The 20th Century Children's Poetry Treasury*

*Lesson example provided in this chapter. Example lessons for the other weeks are on the DVD. Lesson planners for all weeks to use with your own books are also on the DVD.

Figure 4–4 Spring Lessons: March–May, Weeks 19–27 (continues)

Spring Lessons: March–May, Weeks 26–27

Week	New Activities	Repeat Activities	Exemplar Books
26		Discuss text Explore vocabulary Track print while reading Write a sentence interactively For a C-V-C word from the story, write more words that belong to same family	*Caterpillar*
		Identify, give sounds for lower- and uppercase letters I–P	*Babar's ABC*
		Explore rhyme	*The 20th Century Children's Poetry Treasury*
27		Discuss text Explore vocabulary Track print while reading Write a sentence interactively For a C-V-C word from the story, write more words that belong to same family	*Caterpillar*
		Identify, give sounds for lower- and uppercase letters Q–Z	*Babar's ABC*
		Explore rhyme	*The 20th Century Children's Poetry Treasury*

*Lesson example provided in this chapter. Example lessons for the other weeks are on the DVD. Lesson planners for all weeks to use with your own books are also on the DVD.

Figure 4–4 Spring Lessons: March–May, Weeks 19–27 (continued)

New Activity: *Point to, say, and blend three letters in sound boxes that represent the phonemes of a word*

Repeat Activities: *Discuss test; explore vocabulary; act out text; write a sentence interactively*

First read the story just for fun. Briefly discuss the meanings of useful but unfamiliar words as you read: *tag-along, court, play serious ball.*

Discussion: "How do you think Jamaica felt when she went to the park and watched her brother? Why do you think this? How did Jamaica change when she was playing in the sand and the little boy came by? Do you have older brothers or sisters? Tell us about them. Have you ever felt left out because you were too young?" Have students share with a partner and let one or two students share their ideas.

Pointing to letters representing sounds. Pass out filled-in sound box sheets (see Figure 4–5). "I'm going to say several words from the story. See if you can tell me what each one is. Then we'll trace each word on our papers." Read the second page of the story. "What's this word—/g/ /o/ /t/? Yes, *got.* Now let's put our finger on the number one. In the first box next to number one, trace the letter *g* which is the letter for the sound you hear first in /g/ot. In the next box, trace the letter *o*, which is the letter for the sound you hear next in /g/ /o/ /t/. In the last box, trace the letter *t*, which is the letter for the sound you hear at the end of *got*—/g/ /o/ /t/, *got.*" After reading page 6, follow the same procedure with *rim*.

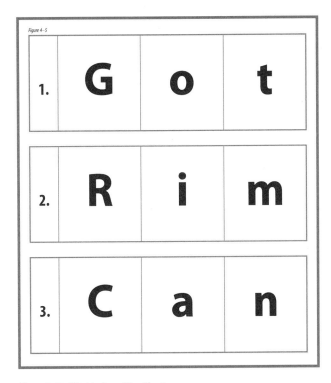

Figure 4–5 Filled-In Sound Box Sheet

Talk about the word *rim*. "What does the word *rim* mean?" After reading page 7 follow the same procedure for *can*. "Put your pencils down. Put your finger by number one. Run your finger under each sound like this as we say the word: /g/ /o/ /t/, *got*." Do the same for *rim* and *can*.

Summarizing narrative text by writing sentences interactively: Write three sentences as a group that summarize the story's beginning (the main character and problem), middle (what happens next), and end (how the problem got solved). Hand out a sheet on which the beginning of each sentence is provided:

Jamaica's brother _____ [*did not let her play*].

Jamaica and Berto _____ [*played in the sand*].

Ossie played in the sand too and Jamaica _____ [*was happy*].

Have children give you as many of the sounds in the words and letters for those sounds as they can. Have them write at least one of the sentences with you as you write it on a chart or whiteboard. Discuss the author's message: *It is nice to let others join in.*

For children who need extra help: Each day reread part of *Jamaica Tag-Along* and work on pointing, saying, and blending three letters in sound boxes that represent a word, just as you did in the whole-group lesson. Also write a sentence interactively (one of the sentences you used in the large group or a different one). Ask some of the same questions and talk about vocabulary that you covered in the whole-group lesson.

Week 20
Book: *Jamaica and Briana*

New Activity: *Write letters of three-phoneme words in sound boxes*

Repeat Activities: *Discuss text; explore vocabulary; say words by blending three phonemes you pronounce in isolation; segment beginning, middle, and ending sounds in a three-phoneme word; write a sentence interactively*

First read the story just for fun. Briefly discuss the meanings of useful but unfamiliar words as you read: *scrunched, copied, drifts of snow.*

Discussion: "Why didn't Jamaica and Briana like their boots? Why did Briana tell Jamaica her new boots were ugly? Did you ever get some new clothes that you really liked? Why did you like them? Where did you wear them? Tell a partner about it." Let a few students share their ideas.

Writing letters in sound boxes: Pass out blank sound box sheets (see Figure 4–6 and on the DVD), as well as alphabet cards children can use to help them write the letters. "I'm going to say several words from the story. See if you can tell me what each one is. Then we'll write each word in sound boxes on our paper." Page 2: "What word is this from the story—/f/ /i/ /t/. Yes, *fit*. Now, let's put our finger on the number one. What sound do you hear first? Yes, /f/. Does anyone know what letter makes this sound? Yes, *f*. In the first box next to number one write the letter *f*, which is the letter for the sound you hear first in *fit*—/f/*it*. What do you hear next in *fit*? Yes, /i/, the short *i* sound that you also hear at the beginning of *insect* on our short vowel chart. In the next box, write the letter *i*.

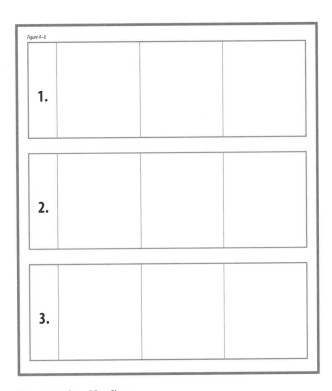

Figure 4–6
1.
2.
3.

Figure 4–6 Sound Box Sheet

What sound do you hear at the end of *fit*? Yes, /t/. Does anyone know what letter makes this sound? Yes, *t*. In the last box, write the letter *t*, which is the letter for the sound you hear at the end of fit—/f/ /i/ /t/." Repeat the same steps for *bus* (page 3) and *tan* (page 7). "Put your pencils down. Put your finger by number one. Run your finger under each sound like this as we say the word /f/ /i/ /t/, *fit*." Do the same with *bus* and *tan*.

Interactive writing: Write one or two sentences about the story together. Have children give as many of the sounds in the words and letters for those sounds as they can. If children are able, have them write one of the sentences with you as you write on a chart. Remember to use the short vowel chart as needed.

Additional Book for Week 20: *Just Grandpa and Me*

Repeat Activities: *Say words by blending three phonemes you pronounce; discuss text; explore vocabulary*

First read the story just for fun. As you read, briefly talk about the meaning of useful but unfamiliar words, such as *suit, revolving door, escalator, chopsticks*.

Discussion: "How do you think the mother felt about the new suit? Do you have a grandparent, aunt, or uncle whom you like to do things with? Tell a partner about it." Let one or two students share their ideas.

As you reread the story, stop and give the phonemes of the following words and see if the children can tell you what they are: (page 1) /n/ /ē/ /d/, *need*; (page 4) /p/ /o/ /p/, *pop*; (page 5) /b/ /i/ /g/, *big*; (page 10) /s/ /ü/ /t/, *suit*. Finish the story.

For children who need extra help: Each day reread part of *Just Grandpa and Me* and work on blending three phonemes into a word, just as you did in the whole-group lesson. Also work on writing words in sound boxes and interactive writing (the same sentence you used for *Jamaica and Briana* in the large group or a different one). Ask some of the same questions and talk about vocabulary that you covered in the whole-group lesson.

New Activity: *Hear the two parts in two-syllable words*

Repeat Activities: *Observe teacher pointing to each word while reading a story summary; recognize that readers read left to right, with a return sweep to the next line; act out text; discuss text; explore vocabulary*

First read the story just for fun. As you read, briefly talk about the meaning of useful but unfamiliar words: *snooze, hoeing, ripe, ground into flour, batter, eager.* Then act out the story. Switch roles and act it out again. On subsequent rereadings, let the children chime in on the chorus.

Discussion: "What lesson did the cat, dog, and mouse learn?" Have children share ideas with a partner and then discuss this as a group. "What is something that smells good to you when it's cooking?"

Hearing both parts of two-syllable words, tracking print while reading, and recognizing that readers read left to right with a return sweep to the next line below: Have the children look at the story summary for *The Little Red Hen* (Figure 4–7 and on the DVD) as you read it to them. "I want to show you how readers can use their finger to point to each word as they read. Here's a sentence from the story: *A cat, dog, mouse, and little red hen lived in a cozy house.*" Read the sentence again and point to each word as you read. "*Little* is one word, so we point to just one word when we read *little. Cozy* is also one word, so we point to just one word when we read *cozy.*" Read the second sentence while tracking the print. Read the

---

The Little Red Hen

Illustrated by

_____

A cat, dog, mouse, and little red hen lived in a cozy house.

The cat, dog, and mouse would not help the hen.

The little red hen did all the work and ate all the bread.

The cat, dog, and mouse became good helpers to get some bread next time.

Figure 4–7 Story Summary of The Little Red Hen

third sentence and talk about *little* again. Read the fourth sentence while track-ing the print. Talk about *became* and *helpers*. Have the children try to track the print on their own copy of the story if you think they are ready. Let them illus-trate their little book and take it home to read to their parents.

Additional Book for Week 21: *Wild Bears*

New Activity: *Summarize informational text by writing a sentence interactively*

Repeat Activities: *Discuss text; explore vocabulary; write three-phoneme words in sound boxes; blend three phonemes in sound boxes to read words in isolation*

Read the book, a few pages a day. This activity will take one week at least.

Discussion: "What did you learn about bears? What fact interested you? Why? What else do you hope to learn about bears?"

Vocabulary: Briefly talk about the meaning of useful but unfamiliar words such as *mammal, thirty miles an hour, great sense of smell, hibernate, den, Asian, Arctic, India, South America, bamboo, china, nature, future*.

 Using sound boxes: Pass out blank sound box sheets (Figure 4–6 and on the DVD), as well as alphabet charts children can refer to when writing letters in the sound boxes. Have the short vowel chart ready to use. "I'm going to say some words from the story. See if you can tell me the word. Then, we'll write it on paper." For example:

> Page 5 (grizzly bear running): "What word is this—/r/ /u/ /n/? Yes, *run*. What sound do you hear at the beginning of *run*? Yes, /r/. Does anyone know what letter makes that sound? Yes, *r*. Now let's put our fingers on the number one. In the first box next to the number one, write the letter *r*, which is the letter for the sound you hear first in *run*—/r/ /u/ /n/, *run*. What do you hear next in *run*? Yes, short *u*, like the sound of the *u* in *umbrella* on our short vowel chart. In the next box, write the letter *u*. What do you hear at the end of run? Yes, /n/. In the last box, write the letter *n*, which is the letter for the sound you hear at the end of *run*—r/u/n/, *run*.

> Page 13 (North American baby cubs): "What word is this—/d/ /e/ /n/? Yes, *den*. What sound do you hear at the beginning of *den*? Yes, /d/. Does anyone know what letter makes that sound? Yes, *d*. Now let's put our finger on the number two. In the first box next to number two, write the letter *d*, which is the letter for the sound you hear first in *den*—/d/ /e/ /n/, *den*. What do you hear next in *den*? Yes, short *e*. In the next box, write the letter *e*, which is the letter for the sound you hear next in /d/ /e/ /n/, *den*. What sound do you hear at the end of *den*? Yes, /n/. In the last box, write the letter that goes with the sound /n/, which is the sound you hear at the end of *den*—/d/e/n/, *den*.

> Page 26 (spectacled bears): Give the sounds /n/ /ə/ /t/ /s/, *nuts*. This time, don't have the children call out the sounds. "Don't say the answer out loud. In the first box by number

three, try to write the letter that you hear at the beginning of *nuts*." Check on the children's progress and provide support as needed. "Now what do you hear in the middle of *nuts*? Yes, short *u*. In the middle box, write the letter *u*, which is the letter for the sound / ə / that you hear in the middle of *nuts*. Again, without saying the answer out loud, in the third box, try to write the letter for the sound that you hear next in *nuts*." Check on the children's progress and provide support as needed. "Now what do you hear at the end of *nuts*? In the last box, try to write the letter you hear at the end of *nuts*." Check on the children's progress and provide support as needed. "Put your pencils down. Put your finger by number one. Run your finger under each sound like this as we say the word, /r/u/n/, *run*." Do the same for *den* and *nuts*.

Summarize informational text using interactive writing: Write one sentence about the last page of *Wild Bears* as students write on their own sheet. Have children give as many of the sounds in the words and letters for those sounds as they can. "Let's come up with one sentence that summarizes the last page of our book. This should tell the most important idea." Lead them to a sentence like, *We need to let bears live in the woods*. It may take you more than one day to write the summary sentence. After students have written along with you, have them track the print as they reread the summary sentence.

For children who need extra help: Each day reread the story summary of *The Little Red Hen* and help students track the print as they read, just as you did in the whole-group lesson. Also reread *Wild Bears* and write words in sound boxes and write a summary sentence interactively (the same sentence you used for *Wild Bears* in the large group or a different one). Ask some of the same questions and talk about vocabulary that you covered in the whole-group lesson.

Week 22

Book: *Ant*

New Activity: *Track print while reading, pointing to each word as it is read and not confusing two-syllable words for two words*

Repeat Activities: *Recognize directionality in reading (left to right, down, and to the left); discuss text; explore vocabulary; segment beginning, middle, and end sounds in two- and three-phoneme words; write sounds in sound boxes; blend three phonemes in sound boxes to read words in isolation; write interactively*

Read pages 4–9. Briefly discuss the meanings of useful but unfamiliar words as you read. Point out words in bold print, the glossary, and the index.

Discussion after pages 6–7: "Describe the ants you have seen. How did you feel about them? Share with a partner." Let one or two students share ideas with the larger group.

Discussion after pages 8–9: "What did you learn about ants today? What else would you like to learn? Let's see if we find out. Share with a partner." Let one or two students share ideas with the larger group.

Using sound boxes: Have children write a few words from the book about ants on a sound box sheet (see Figure 4–6 and on the DVD). Have the short vowel chart ready to use. Reread page 4. "What sound do you hear first in *six*—/s/*ix*. Yes, /s/. Does anyone know what letter this sound is? Yes, *s*. Write it in the first box by the number one. What is the next sound you hear in *six*? Yes, /i/. This is spelled with the letter *i*. Write it in the second box by number one. What is the last sound you hear in *six*? Yes, /x/. Does anyone know what letter makes this sound? Yes, *x*. Write *x* in the last box by number one." Go on to the word *leg*, also on page 4. This time, don't have the children take turns calling out the sound. "Without saying the answer out loud, in the first box by number two, try to write the letter that you hear at the beginning of /l/ /e/ /g/, *leg*." Check on the children's progress and provide support as needed. "Now what do you hear in the middle of /l/ /e/ /g/? In the middle box of number two, write the letter *e*, which is the letter for the sound that you hear in the middle of /l/ /e/ /g/, *leg*. Again, without saying the answer out loud, in the third box of number two, try to write the letter for the sound that you hear at the end of /l/ /e/ /g/, *leg*." Check on the children's progress and provide support as needed.

Tracking print while reading: "I want to show you again how I can use my finger to point to each word as I read." Read the first page of the *Ants* summary (Figure 4–8 and on the DVD), pointing to each word as you read. Point out that *insects* is only one word so you only point to one word when reading it. Then read page 2. "See how I go from this side by my left hand to this side by my right hand?" Point out that *feelers* is only one word so you only point to one word when reading it. Then read page 3. "There are two lines on this page. I go down to the next line by my left side and read across to my right side." Have children try to track the print in their own copy of the summary if you think

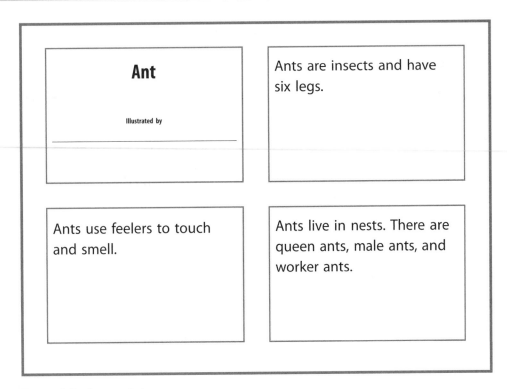

Ant Illustrated by _____	Ants are insects and have six legs.
Ants use feelers to touch and smell.	Ants live in nests. There are queen ants, male ants, and worker ants.

Figure 4–8 Text Summary for Ant

they are ready. Keep in mind that exposure, not mastery, is the objective. Let children illustrate their little book and take it home. Attach the sound box sheet to the back of the story. Tell them they should practice reading their story and sound box words from the story over the summer.

Interactive writing: Write one or two sentences about the text as students write on their own sheet. Have children give as many of the sounds in the words and letters for those sounds as they can.

Additional Book for Week 22:
What Animals Need

Repeat Activities: *Discuss text; explore vocabulary; summarize informational text using interactive writing*

Discuss the text. Talk about vocabulary: *hunt, bison, chameleon, hawk, koala.* Generate a summary. For example: *Animals need food, water, and safety. Baby animals need care.* Have students give you as many of the letters for the sounds in the words as they write along with you. It will take several days to write the summary sentence.

Additional Book for Week 22:
A, My Name Is Alice

Repeat Activities: *Identify upper- and lowercase letters A–H; give sounds for letters A–H*

Reread pages A–H. Have children tell you the names of the upper- and lowercase letters on different days. At the end of each page, have children articulate the sounds made by the letters A, B, C, D, E, F, G, H, giving the short and long sound for each vowel.

Additional Book for Week 22:
The 20th Century Children's Poetry Treasury

Repeat Activities: *Explore rhyme, act out text*

Reread favorite poems. Have the children tell you which words rhyme.

OR

Act out a favorite story from earlier in the year.

For children who need extra help: Each day reread the *Ant* summary and help students track print as they read, just as you did in the whole-group lesson. If necessary, help students finish writing the summary sentences they started with the whole group. Also write words in sound boxes. Ask some of the same questions and talk about vocabulary that you covered in the whole-group lesson. Review letter names and sounds as needed.

New Activity: *Use a C-V-C word from the story to write more words that belong to the same word family*

Repeat Activities: *Discuss text; explore vocabulary; use sound boxes; write a sentence interactively*

Read pages 4–13. Briefly discuss the meanings of useful but unfamiliar words as you read. Point out words in bold type, the glossary, and the index.

Discussion before reading: "Describe the caterpillars you have seen. What do you know about caterpillars? What do you want to learn? Share with a partner." Let one or two students share their ideas with the whole group.

Discussion after reading: "What did you learn about caterpillars? What was one of the facts you learned that you liked a lot? Share with a partner." Let one or two students share their ideas with the whole group.

Using sound boxes: "Let's write a few words from the book about caterpillars on our sound box sheet [see Figure 4–6]." For example:

> Reread page 4. "What sound do you hear first in the word *will* – /w/*ill*. Yes, /w/. Does anyone know what letter makes this sound? Yes, *w*. Write it in the first box by number one. What is the next sound you hear in *will*? Yes, /i/. This is spelled with the letter *i*. Write *i* in the second box by number one. What is the last sound you hear in *will*? Yes, /l/. There are two *l*s at the end of *will*. Write *ll* in the last box by number one."

> Reread page 12. This time, don't have the children take turns calling out the sounds. "Without saying the answer out loud, in the first box by number two, try to write the letter for the sound that you hear at the beginning of /ō/ /l/ /d/, *old*." Check on the children's progress and provide support as needed. "Now what do you hear in the middle of /ō/ /l/ /d/? In the middle box of number two, write the letter *l*, which is the letter for the sound /l/ that you hear in the middle of /ō/l/d/, *old*. Without saying the answer out loud, in the third box of number two, try to write the letter for the sound that you hear at the end of /ō/l/d/, *old*." Check on the children's progress and provide support as needed.

Writing words that belong to the same word family: "Now let's try something new. Let's write words that rhyme with *will* and are from the same family. *Will* ends with the word chunk *ill*. *Bill* also ends with the word chunk *ill* and rhymes with *will*. *Fill* also ends with *ill* and rhymes with *will* and *Bill*. Write *fill* on your whiteboard. Now erase the *f* and add a *k*. What word to you have? Now erase the *k* and write a *p*. What word do you have? In first grade you'll learn a lot more about word families. When you are reading and see a familiar word chunk, this will help you sound out the word. You give the first sound and then say the chunk and you come up with the word." At this point, the work on word families is for exposure, not mastery. Repeat the same sequence with *old*. Students should be able to generate many of the following words: *bold, cold, fold, gold, hold, mold, sold, told*.

Tracking print while reading: Do this on another day. "I want to show you how I can use my finger to point to each word as I read." Read the first page of the *Caterpillar* summary (Figure 4–9 and on the DVD), pointing to each word as you read. "I point to each word as I read. See how I go from this side by my left hand to this side by my right hand." Point out that *caterpillar* is only one word so you only point to one word when you say it. Point out that *butterfly* is only one word. Before reading page 2, ask children how many times you should point to the word *caterpillars*. Read page 2 and say, "I go down to the next line by my left side and read across to my right side." Point out that *bodies* is only one word. Read and track the print on pages 3 and 4 of the summary. Ask the children to tell you how many times to point to the word *caterpillars*. Have children try to track the print on their own copy of the summary if you think they are ready. Keep in mind that exposure, not mastery, is the objective. Let them illustrate their little book and take it home. Attach the sound box sheet to the back of the book. Tell them they should practice reading their book and sound box words from the book over the summer.

Interactive writing: Write one or two sentences about the book as students write on their own sheet. Have children give as many of the sounds in the words and letters for those sounds as they can.

<table>
<tr><td>

Caterpillar

Illustrated by

_____

</td><td>

A caterpillar will turn into a moth or butterfly.

But it needs to grow and change.

</td><td>

Caterpillars have long, thin bodies.

They also have legs.

</td></tr>
<tr><td></td><td>

Caterpillars hatch from eggs.

Then they eat, eat, eat!

</td><td>

When the caterpillar's skin is too small, it molts. Then it grows a new skin.

</td></tr>
</table>

Figure 4–9 Text Summary for Caterpillar

Additional Book for Week 25: *Babar's ABC*

Repeat Activity: *Identify and give sounds for lower- and uppercase letters A–H*

Reread pages A–H. Have children tell you the names of the upper- and lower-case letters on different days. At the end of each page, have children articulate the sound made by A–H, including the short and long sounds for vowels.

Additional Book for Week 25: *The 20th Century Children's Poetry Treasury*

Repeat Activities: *Identify rhyming words; act out text*

Reread favorite poems. Have the children tell you which words rhyme.

OR

Act out a favorite poem or story from earlier in the year.

For children who need extra help: Each day reread the story summary of *Caterpillar* and help students track print as they read, just as you did in the whole-group lesson. Also work on writing words in sound boxes and interactive writing (the same sentence you used in the large group or a different one). Ask some of the same questions and talk about vocabulary that you covered in the whole-group lesson. Review letter names and sounds for A–H as needed.

Chapter Summary

The EIR kindergarten whole-group lessons offer motivating experiences with quality literature to all your emergent readers as well as carefully sequenced phonemic awareness and phonics instruction embedded within these literature experiences. In addition to word work, the lessons focus on developing students' oral language abilities, vocabulary, and comprehension of texts read aloud. The small-group follow-up lessons provide students who need more support with additional opportunities to develop the emergent literacy abilities covered in the whole-group lessons. Now that you have an idea about the content and focus of the weekly lessons, Chapter 5 addresses assessment procedures for selecting students in need of the additional small-group support, for monitoring all students during the year on emergent literacy and oral language abilities covered in EIR lessons, and for assessing students' at the end of the year.

Assessing Kindergartners in EIR

In this chapter, I share fall and spring assessments that will help you determine which of your kindergartners will benefit from supplemental reading instruction as well as provide advice for monitoring their reading progress throughout the year.

Fall Assessments

In September, assess kindergartners who you think may need EIR small-group follow-up support in order to be successful readers in first grade. The assessments are typical of those commonly administered at the beginning of the school year. Research has found that letter name knowledge and phonemic awareness are the best two predictors of end-of-first-grade reading achievement (Adams 1990; Snow et al.1998). In the fall, you'll use students' knowledge of letter names and sounds and their ability to generate words that rhyme with target words (an early phonemic awareness ability), along with your judgment, to decide which students will benefit from small-group EIR support. All assessments are administered individually and are best given in the morning when children are less tired. (Other children can be working independently during this time.)

First, assess students' knowledge of letter names and sounds (see Figure 5–1), which takes 5 or 10 minutes. Next, administer the rhyme test (Figure 5–2), which takes about 5 minutes. (You don't have to do both assessments on the same day.) These assessments are briefly described next. Explicit directions for administering them are provided in Figure 5–3. Figure 5–4 is a summary sheet for recording scores. (All these forms are available on the DVD.)

Letter Name and Letter Sound Assessment

Starting with the column of uppercase letters, ask the child to tell you the names of the letters. Don't offer any help or indicate whether the answer is right or wrong. Record correct responses with a check mark. If the child gives an incorrect response, record the incorrect letter. If the child cannot or will not give a response, record 0. Stop the test if the child is unable to identify ten *consecutive* letters.

Then move to the column of lowercase letters and follow the same procedure.

Finally, go to the column headed *consonant sounds* and ask the child to give you the sound each consonant makes (ask for two sounds for *c* and *g*).

Phonemic Awareness Assessment: Generating Rhyming Words

Say, "Words that rhyme sound the same. *Cat* rhymes with *fat*, *pig* rhymes with *dig*. Can you tell me a word that rhymes with *sun*?" A nonsense word response is okay. If the child is unable to respond, say that *fun* rhymes with *sun*. Present two more practice items before administering the test: "What is a word that rhymes with *sit*?" "What is a word that rhymes with *book*?" Again, if the child can't answer, tell him or her a rhyming word.

Then administer the test (see Figure 5–2) without providing or correcting responses. Write down the student's responses on the test sheet, incorrect as well as correct. The incorrect responses may give you clues about why the child is having difficulty coming up with rhyming words. (Count rhyming nonsense words as correct.)

Looking at Scores to See Which Children May Need EIR

The statistics that follow will help you identify students who will benefit from EIR follow-up lessons. If you are unsure in a particular case, err on the side of putting the child in an EIR support group rather than not. It's better to drop the EIR follow-up lessons later because the child is doing well than for her or him to get further behind without the support.

In a study of a thousand kindergarten students from twenty-three schools (on average, 63 percent of the students received a subsidized lunch and 25 percent were English language learners), children in the fall of kindergarten, on average, knew thirty-two letter names (upper- and lowercase combined) and seven consonant sounds (Taylor 2010d). In the spring of first grade, children in the lowest third of this group (that is, who knew twenty letter names,

Letter Name and Letter Sound Assessment

Letter Name—Uppercase*	Letter Name—Lowercase*	Consonant Sounds**
K	k	k
G	g	g
A	a	g
P	p	p
W	w	w
B	b	b
H	h	h
C	c	c
I	i	c
J	j	j
Y	y	y
L	l	l
Q	q	qu
M	m	m
D	d	d
N	n	n
S	s	s
X	x	x
F	f	f
Z	z	z
R	r	r
V	v	v
T	t	t
E	e	
O	o	
U	u	

*Check if known
**Check if known (ask for two different sounds for g and c)

Total Uppercase Letters Correct _____   Total Lowercase Letters Correct _____

Combined Total Correct _____

Total Consonant Sounds Correct _____

Figure 5–1 Letter Name and Letter Sound Assessment

Kindergarten Rhyme Test

Directions: Say, "Tell me a word that rhymes with [use each word in the list below]."
Nonsense words are okay.

Test Items	Student Responses
1. man	_____
2. red	_____
3. sick	_____
4. top	_____
5. duck	_____
6. play	_____
7. light	_____
8. me	_____

Total Rhymes Correct _____

Figure 5–2 Kindergarten Rhyme Test

Directions for Fall Assessment

Assessment Date(s): _____

Step 1. Administer the letter name portion of the assessment.

a. Begin with the uppercase letters. Say, "I'd like you to tell me the names of these letters. What letter is this?" (You may point to the letter.)

b. Do not provide any help or indicate whether the answer is right or wrong.

c. Record correct responses with a check mark. If the child gives an incorrect response, record the incorrect letter. If the child cannot or will not give a response, record 0.

d. Stop the test if a child is unable to identify ten *consecutive* letters.

e. Repeat the process with the lowercase letters.

f. Record the total number of correctly identified upper- and lowercase letters.

Step 2. Administer the consonant sound portion of the assessment.

a. Say, "I'd like you to tell me the sounds of these letters. What sound does this letter make?" (You may point to the letter.) For g and c, ask for the two common sounds each letter makes.

b. Do not provide any help or reveal whether the answer is right or wrong.

c. Record the correct response with a check mark. If the child gives an incorrect response, record the incorrect sound. If the child cannot or will not give a response, record 0.

d. Stop the test if a child is unable to identify ten *consecutive* sounds.

e. Record the number of correctly identified letter sounds.

Step 3. Conduct the rhyme test as directed.

If the child gives a nonsense word that rhymes with the prompt, *count it correct*. For example, *dat* rhymes with *bat* even though it is not a real word.

Step 4. Record the child's name and the number of correct responses on the fall assessment summary sheet.

Figure 5–3 Directions for Fall Assessment

Kindergarten Fall Summary Sheet

Teacher: _____   Date: _____

Student	Uppercase Letter Names	Lowercase Letter Names	Total Letter Names	Consonant Sounds	Rhymes

Figure 5–4 Kindergarten Fall Summary Sheet

upper- and lowercase combined, and three consonant sounds when they started kindergarten) were reading thirty words per minute correctly and had a normal curve equivalent (NCE) of 33 in decoding and 28 in comprehension on a standardized reading test. In general, then, kindergartners who knew twenty or fewer upper- and lowercase letter names and only a few consonant sounds and who do not understand the concept of rhyme need small-group follow-up EIR support.

Assessing Students' Reading Progress During the School Year

Regular assessment of students' progress is also embedded in EIR instruction. Figure 5–5 is a checklist of emergent reading skills that are stressed in kindergarten EIR lessons. Three times between the EIR fall assessment and the EIR spring assessment, decide for each skill listed whether the child demonstrates good or average ability or needs support. For more information on kindergarten assessments, standards, and benchmarks, see the Common Core State Standards (at www.corestandards.org/the-standards/english-language-arts-standards), Resnick and Hampton (2009) and McGee and Morrow (2005).

Assessment Checklist of Kindergarten Emergent Literacy Skills

Three times during the year, after the initial fall assessment and before the end-of-year spring assessment, rate a child's ability in each emergent literacy skill as G (good), A (average), or N (needs support).

Student: _____

Notes	Skill	Fall	Winter	Spring
	Phonemic Awareness			
	Identifies rhyming words			
	Produces rhyming words			
	Hears the beginning sound in a word			
	Identifies pictures of things that begin with a particular sound			
	Hears the beginning sound in a word			
	Hears the ending sound in a word			
	Segments the sounds in words with two phonemes (C-V or V-C)			
	Segments the sounds in three-phoneme words			
	Blends two phonemes to make a word			
	Blends three phonemes to make a word			
	Phonics			
	Identifies lower- and uppercase letters			
	Writes lower- and uppercase letters			
	Identifies sounds for consonants			
	Identifies long and short sounds for vowels			
	Identifies words that begin with a particular sound			
	Writes words in sound boxes			
	Writes a sentence interactively			
	Writes words from same word family			

Notes	Skill	Fall	Winter	Spring
	Concepts of Print/Decoding			
	Identifies (hears number of) words in a sentence			
	Understands that readers read left to right, with a return sweep to the next line			
	Tracks print while reading			
	Hears two parts in a two-syllable word and tracks it as one word			
	Vocabulary			
	Learns new vocabulary in texts read based on discussions			
	Is interested in new vocabulary			
	Creative Drama/Oral Language			
	Participates in acting out stories/texts			
	Is interested in creative drama			
	Comprehension/Oral Language: Talking and Writing About Text			
	Answers detailed questions about texts read			
	Answers interpretive questions about texts read			
	Makes connections to texts read			
	Independently writes words and draws pictures about texts read			
	Independently writes one or more sentences about texts read			
	Comprehension Strategies			
	Participates in summarizing narratives			
	Participates in summarizing informational text			

Figure 5–5 *Assessment Checklist of Kindergarten Emergent Literacy Skills*

Taking a Child Out of EIR

The guidelines that follow can help you decide whether a child no longer requires EIR small-group follow-up support. In general, be conservative: don't remove a child from the group too quickly. Also, watch closely to see whether children you have released are making good progress in the regular program. If not, they should rejoin the EIR group.

Criteria for Taking a Child Out of EIR

> ▶ The child has had EIR small-group lessons for at least three months.

> ▶ The child is clearly ahead of other children in the group.

> ▶ The child is performing effectively in grade-level texts and tasks in the classroom.

> ▶ The child knows almost all the letter names and letter sounds.

> ▶ The child demonstrates phonemic awareness by segmenting and blending some C-V-C words on the phonemic awareness test (see Figure 5–6).

Spring Assessments

In the spring, you'll use kindergartners' knowledge of letter names and sounds and their ability to segment and blend phonemes, along with your judgment, to determine whether they may need additional early reading intervention in first grade. In May, re-administer the letter name and consonant sound test you gave in the fall. Don't re-administer the rhyme test. Instead, use the phonemic awareness test (see Figures 5–6 to 5–8), which assesses a student's ability to blend individual sounds into words and hear the individual sounds in words.

The Phonemic Awareness Test

The goal of the kindergarten EIR program is to prepare children to become independent readers in grade 1. In the spring, you should use the phonemic awareness test to assess students' ability to segment and blend the sounds in three- or four-phoneme words and identify children who may need supplemental reading instruction in first grade. The test takes about 10 minutes to administer.

Children who score 5 or less on this twelve-item test in September of first grade are at considerable risk of failing to learn to read during the school year (Taylor 1991). Those who score 8 or more have an excellent chance of reading well by the end of the year. (Additional information on how to administer this test, along with information on its reliability and validity are provided on the DVD; see "A Test of Phonemic Awareness for Classroom Use.")

The cut-off scores of 5 or below and 8 or above on the Phonemic Segmentation and Blending Test were determined from assessments made in September of first grade and based on the description of test administration procedures provided in the paper. If you administer the test more leniently (e.g., provide correct responses to missed items as you go through the test), I cannot tell you how to interpret the scores. However, in schools in which teachers use the EIR

TIPS FOR ADMINISTERING THE PHONEMIC AWARENESS TEST

▶ *Pronounce each word naturally.* In the blending portion of the test, pronounce each sound but exaggerate the sounds as little as possible.

▶ *Practice with a colleague.* Before giving the test to children, give it to each other.

▶ *Practice on a proficient kindergarten student.* Practicing with a student who you know will do well builds your confidence that you are administering the test properly. (When a less skilled child does poorly on the test, you will be less likely to think the weak performance is due to faulty test administration.)

▶ If a child can't respond to your practice blending statement, tell her the word and then review the practice statement, pronouncing each sound but exaggerating the sounds as little as possible. However, don't provide the answers for items missed on the test itself.

▶ Begin the segmentation portion of the test by going over the example. Say, "What sound do you hear first in *sad*? What sound do you hear next in *sad*? What sound do you hear at the end of *sad*?" If a child can't do this, do it for him. If you need to, you can return to the practice item to review what the child is to do, but do not provide answers for items missed on the test. Also, if you need to, you can continue to say throughout the test, "What do you hear first in *pat*? What do you hear next in *pat*? What do you hear at the end of *pat*?" If a child gives you the letter name, say this is correct but ask for the sound the letter makes. Demonstrate again that the first sound in *sad* is /s/, the second sound is /ă/, and the end sound is /d/.

kindergarten program, this test also accurately predicts end-of-first-grade reading achievement when administered in the spring of kindergarten (Taylor 2010f). (In addition, many children grow in phonemic awareness from the end of kindergarten to the beginning of first grade.)

Interpreting Spring Scores

In the study of one thousand kindergarten students from 23 schools (Taylor, 2011b), children in the spring of kindergarten, on average, knew 48 letter names (upper- and lowercase) and eighteen consonant sounds and had a mean phonemic awareness score of 7.5. Children who were in the lowest third of this group by the end of first grade (reading 30 words per minute correctly; had a normal curve equivalent (NCE) of 33 in decoding and 28 in comprehension on a standardized reading test in spring of first grade) knew, on average, 43 upper- and lowercase letter names and 16 consonant sounds, and had a phonemic awareness score of 4.8 at the end of kindergarten. Table 5–1 charts indicators of good, average, and below-average progress in letter-name

Phonemic Awareness Test

Name: _____   **Teacher:** _____

Blending Assessment

Example: "When I say /c/ /a/ /b/, can you tell me the word?"

1.	Say /t/ /a/ /p/		
2.	Say /s/ /e/ /t/		
3.	Say /f/ /i/ /b/		
4.	Say /j/ /o/ /g/		
5.	Say /c/ /a/ /t/		
6.	Say /s/ /o/ /f/ /t/		

Number Correct _____

Segmentation Assessment

Example: "When I say *sad*, can you give each sound you hear in the word?"

7.	Say *pat*		
8.	Say *bet*		
9.	Say *sip*		
10.	Say *pod*		
11.	Say *tub*		
12.	Say *fast*		

Number Correct _____

Figure 5–6 Phonemic Awareness Test

Directions for Spring Assessments

Step 1. Administer the letter name portion of the assessment.
   a. Begin with the uppercase letters. Say, "I'd like you to tell me the names of these letters. What letter is this?" (You may point to the letter.)
   b. Do not provide any help or indicate whether the answer is right or wrong.
   c. Record correct responses with a check mark. If the child gives an incorrect response, record the incorrect letter. If the child cannot or will not give a response, record 0.
   d. Stop the test if a child is unable to identify ten *consecutive* letters.
   e. Repeat the process with the lowercase letters.
   f. Record the total number of correctly identified upper- and lowercase letters.

Step 2. Administer the consonant sound portion of the assessment.
   a. Say, "I'd like you to tell me the sounds of these letters. What sound does this letter make?" (You may point to the letter.) For *g* and *c*, ask for the two common sounds each letter makes.
   b. Do not provide any help or reveal whether the answer is right or wrong.
   c. Record the correct response with a check mark. If the child gives an incorrect response, record the incorrect sound. If the child cannot or will not give a response, record 0.
   d. Stop the test if a child is unable to identify ten *consecutive* sounds.
   e. Record the number of correctly identified letter sounds.

Step 3. Administer the blending section of the phonemic awareness test.
   a. Present the example. Say, "I am going to give you some sounds and I would like you to put the sounds together into a word. For example, when I say /c/ /a/ /b/, can you tell me the word?" If the child is unable to respond or responds incorrectly, complete the practice item: "The sounds /c/ /a/ /b/ go together to make the word *cab*. Now you try the next one."
   b. Have the child respond to items 1–6:
      • After each item, write the child's response.
      • If the response is incorrect or the child is unable to do the item, do *not* correct the child or do the task correctly. (You may return to the practice item, however.)
      • An item must be totally correct to be scored correct. For example, for number 2, if the child says *sat* for *set*, the item is incorrect.
   c. Record the number of correct responses.

Step 4. Administer the segmentation section of the phonemic awareness text.
   a. Present the example. Say, "I am going to say some words and I would like you to give me the sound that you hear first in the word, the sound that you hear next, and the sound that you hear at the end of the word. For example, when I say *sad*, can you give each sound that you hear in the word? What sound do you hear first in *sad*? What sound do you hear next in *sad*? What sound do you hear at the end of *sad*?" If the child is unable to respond or responds incorrectly, complete the practice item: "The sound at the beginning of *sad* is /s/, the next sound is /_/, and the sound at the end of *sad* is /d/."
   b. Have the child complete items 7–12.
      • If the response is incorrect or the child is unable to do the task, do *not* correct the child or complete the task yourself. (You may return to the practice item, however.)
      • An item must be totally correct to be scored correct. For example, if for item 8, *bet*, the child says /b/ /e/ /d/, the response is incorrect.
   c. Record the number of correct responses.

Step 5. Transfer all information to the spring summary sheet.

Figure 5–7 Directions for Spring Assessments

Kindergarten Spring Summary Sheet

Date of Assessments: _____

Student	Total Letter Name Score	Consonant Sound Score	Phoneme Blending Score (PB)	Phoneme Segmentation Score (PS)	PB + PS Score	Possibly in EIR in fall of grade 1 (check)

Figure 5–8 Kindergarten Spring Summary Sheet

Indicators of Phonemic Awareness and Phonics Knowledge in Kindergarten Assessments

	May be in need of a systematic early reading intervention program	Making adequate progress in phonics knowledge and phonemic awareness	Demonstrates above-average in phonics knowledge and phonemic awareness
Fall	Knows fewer than 20 letter names Knows 3 or fewer consonant sounds Produces no rhymes	Knows between 20 and 40 letter names Knows at least 4 but fewer than 10 consonant sounds Completes a few rhymes	Knows 40 or more letter names Knows 10 or more consonant sounds Completes most rhymes
Spring	Scores 5 or lower on phonemic awareness test Knows fewer than 45 letter names Knows fewer than 15 consonant sounds	Scores higher than 7 and lower than 10 on phonemic awareness test Knows between 45 and 50 letter names Knows between 15 and 20 consonant sounds	Scores higher than 10 on phonemic awareness test Knows more than 50 letter names Knows more than 20 consonant sounds

Table 5–1   Indicators of Phonemic Awareness and Phonics Knowledge in Kindergarten Assessments

knowledge, consonant sound knowledge, and phonemic segmentation and blending ability in the fall and spring of kindergarten.

In general, students in your class whose scores, in the spring, on the letter name, consonant sound, and phonemic awareness tests are in the lowest quarter or third—or who know fewer than 45 letter names, fewer than 15 consonant sounds, and have a score of 5 or lower on the phonemic awareness test—will likely need additional small-group EIR support in the fall of first grade (Taylor 2010a).

Summary

Watching students closely as they tackle the complex task of learning to read is imperative so that your teaching can be informed by what students know and are able to do, as well by your understanding of what is causing them difficulties. Assessing your students' emergent reading abilities and comprehension at the beginning and end of the school year and at regular points during your weekly EIR lessons offers all of your students, in particular your struggling readers, the best possible chances for success.

Managing Your Reading Block with EIR

ow do EIR lessons fit into your reading, reading/writing, or literacy block? Teachers set up their literacy instruction in ways that suit their individual teaching styles and students' needs, and EIR lessons can be incorporated into any effective iteration. However, some components are always present: whole-group instruction, small-group instruction (including guided reading and EIR lessons), and independent reading/activities for your students while you are working with small groups.

Take a look at your reading block schedule. Research shows that effective teachers *balance* whole-class and small-group instruction (Pressley et al. 2002; Taylor et al. 2007). My research also shows that spending too much time on whole-group instruction (60 percent of the time or more) or too much time on small-group instruction (85 percent of the time or more) negatively affects students' reading development (Taylor et al. 2000; Taylor et al. 2007).

With this necessary balance in mind, it's often most powerful to begin the reading block with a whole-group lesson in which you provide explicit instruction in a reading skill or strategy using a high-quality trade book or literature from a basal reader anthology. That is, you teach the reading skill in the context of students enjoying a story or piece of nonfiction. Then you differentiate your instruction, including a follow-up small-group lesson on the skill or strategy covered in the whole-group lesson (Taylor 2011b). You, and in turn your students, need to be aware of the connection between whole-group, small-group, and one-on-one instruction; it should not be a hidden thread but a visible thread. Students are in a much better position to learn when you point out the connection explicitly. For example, Lena Jacobson reads *Penguin Rescue*, a nonfiction text about saving penguins from an oil spill, to her class in the morning. They discuss the text and the author's messages: "The ship driver should have tried not to hit the rock. Then the oil wouldn't have spilled and hurt the penguins," and "You can help out animals that need it." Then Lena coaches the students to summarize: "It's about penguins and how they got rescued from oil."

In small guided reading groups later that morning, Lena revisits summarizing as the students read informational books at their emergent reading levels. She differentiates her instruction based on students' abilities. In one group of higher-level readers, Lena has students read their book on their own (they had read it together the day before) and then write a group summary sentence individually as Lena coaches them to come up with (but does not tell them) the letters that go with the sounds of the words in their sentence. The average readers in another group also write the group summary sentence as Lena coaches

Helpful Resources

Fountas, I. C., and G. S. Pinnell. 1996. *Guided Reading: Good First Teaching for All Children*. Portsmouth, NH: Heinemann.

Lapp, D., D. Fisher, and T. D. Wolsey. 2009. *Literacy Growth for Every Child: Differentiated Small-Group Instruction, K–6*. New York: Guilford.

Manning, M., G. Morrison, and D. Camp. 2009. *Creating the Best Literacy Block Ever*. New York: Scholastic.

McGee, L. M., and L. M. Morrow. 2005. *Teaching Literacy in Kindergarten*. New York: Guilford.

Pressley, M. 2006. *Reading Instruction That Works: The Case for Balanced Teaching*, 3d ed. New York: Guilford.

Pressley, M., S. E. Dolezal, L. M. Raphael, L. Mohan, A. D. Roehrig, and K. Bogner. 2003. *Motivating Primary-Grade Students*. New York: Guilford.

Routman, R. 2003. *Reading Essentials*. Portsmouth, NH: Heinemann.

———. 2008. *Teaching Essentials*. Portsmouth, NH: Heinemann.

Taberski, S. 2000. *On Solid Ground: Strategies for Teaching Reading K–3*. Portsmouth, NH: Heinemann.

Tyner, B. 2009. *Small-Group Reading Instruction: A Differentiated Teaching Model for Beginning and Struggling Readers*. Newark, DE: International Reading Association.

Walpole, S., and M. C. McKenna. 2009. *How to Plan Differentiated Reading Instruction: Resources for Grades K–3*. New York: Guilford.

Key Classroom Practices

Effective teachers use good classroom management practices (Pressley et al. 2003). There are many excellent professional books listed in this chapter that can help you develop and manage a dynamic literacy block, but here are a few key components:

▶ During the first week, jointly with your students, establish classroom rules and routines to minimize disruptions and provide smooth transitions within and between lessons.

▶ Review classroom rules during the morning meeting.

▶ Use positive language and provide a motivating, engaging environment.

▶ Make a conscious effort to develop self-regulated, independent learners.

▶ Give specific, constructive feedback to students regularly, provide encouragement, and challenge them to think more deeply.

▶ Ask students to evaluate their actions after a discussion or activity, focusing on strengths and areas in need of improvement.

▶ Demonstrate enthusiasm for learning and set high expectations for your students.

▶ Show students that you care about them as individuals, but also let them know that you will be firm, holding them to high standards as learners and good citizens.

▶ Teach students how to compliment one another and encourage them to respect one another.

▶ Offer sincere praise to students, as a group or individually, when they follow classroom and school policies.

▶ Have a brief class meeting at the end of the day and ask students how they thought they behaved that day.

them, but they have read an easier book chorally, not on their own. The children in the below-average group read a very simple book chorally, and Lena provides more support when they are writing their group summary sentence, giving them the letters for sounds when necessary.

Reading Block Schedules: Examples of Effective Balance

The three teachers you met in Chapter 2 typically start their reading block with a 20- or 30-minute whole-group lesson (broken up with brief partner work) and later in the morning have a 10- or 15-minute EIR whole-group lesson.

They provide 20 or 30 minutes of differentiated instruction to various small groups, depending on students' reading abilities and needs. All three teachers also provide 10-minute EIR follow-up lessons to their struggling readers. They explicitly state their lesson purposes in both whole- and small-group lessons. They move at an efficient pace, guided by lesson goals, and meet with as many small groups as possible. Each teacher's schedule is included here along with a brief discussion of how the reading block might be structured.

Choua's Daily Reading Block Schedule

9:00–9:25	Whole-Group Minilesson
9:30–9:45	Small Group 1
9:50–10:05	Small Group 2
10:10–10:25	Small Group 3
10:30–10:45	EIR Whole-Group Lesson
10:50–11:00	EIR Small-Group Follow-Up

Choua has a 120-minute reading block. She spends about 25 minutes a day on a whole-group lesson related to the core reading program and 15 minutes on an EIR emergent literacy lesson. She spends about an hour a day on three guided reading groups using leveled texts and 10 minutes on one EIR group (a second dose of quality small-group instruction for students who need more support). Her average and above-average readers spend about 50 minutes a day on independent learning activities that include independent reading. Her below-average readers get a 10-minute EIR follow-up lesson and spend about 40 minutes a day on independent learning activities. Typically, the below-average readers divide their time among three independent activities. She has a parent or senior citizen volunteer in her classroom during her reading instruction.

Stan's Daily Reading Block Schedule

9:00–9:25	Whole-Group Minilesson
9:30–9:50	Small Group 1
9:50–10:10	Small Group 2
10:10–10:30	Small Group 3
12:15–12:30	Whole-Class EIR Lesson
12:30–12:40	EIR Small-Group Lesson

Stan has a 115-minute reading block. Stan begins with a whole-group lesson that lasts about 25 minutes. He then spends about an hour on three guided reading groups. After lunch he spends 15 minutes on an EIR whole-group lesson and 10 minutes on a small-group follow-up lesson. During this small-group lesson the other students read independently or complete activities they began in the morning.

Choua's Typical Daily Reading Block at a Glance

Whole-Group Lesson (25 minutes on core reading program and 15 minutes on EIR lesson)	Small-Group Lessons (15 minutes for each group using leveled texts)	EIR Small-Group Lesson (10 minutes)	Group	Independent Activities
Read basal reader selection, target comprehension skill/strategy, teach vocabulary at point of contact, discuss high-level questions, review independent activities	Teach phonemic awareness and phonics as needed, read text and coach on word-recognition strategies, discuss vocabulary at point of contact, provide follow-up to comprehension skill/strategy taught in whole group, discuss high-level questions about leveled text			
X	X		Above-average readers* X	*Activity 1*: Rereading, writing/drawing, discussing, vocabulary work as follow-up to whole-group text
			X	*Activity 2*: Rereading, writing/drawing, discussing, word work as follow-up to whole-group text
			X	*Activity 3*: Rereading, writing/drawing, discussing text unrelated to whole- or small-group lesson
			X	*Activity 4*: Reading for pleasure from books of choice
X	X		Average readers* X	Activity 1
			X	Activity 2
			X	Activity 3
			X	Activity 4
X	X		Below-average readers** X	Activity 1
		X	X	Activity 2 or 3
			X	Activity 4

*10–20 minutes for each activity, for a total of 50 minutes

**10–20 minutes for each activity, for a total of 40 minutes

Lena's Daily Reading Block Schedule

9:15–9:40	Whole-Group Lesson from Core Reading Program
9:45–10:00	Small Group 1
10:05–10:20	Small Group 2
10:25–10:40	Small Group 3
10:45–11:00	EIR Whole-Group Lesson
1:00–1:10	EIR Small-Group Lesson

Lena has a 115-minute reading block. In the morning Lena spends 25 minutes on a whole-group lesson from the core reading program, about 55 minutes with three guided reading groups, and 15 minutes on an EIR whole-group lesson. In the afternoon she spends 10 minutes with her EIR small group. Lena has an educational assistant in her room in the morning to work with students who are working independently. An ELL teacher comes into the classroom for 30 minutes, spending 15 minutes with each of two groups of students.

Independent Activities

The amount of independent work time required, so teachers can spend quality time with small groups, warrants that the independent activities students are engaged in are challenging and motivating. Also, a common question that teachers ask as they embark upon EIR lessons for their struggling readers is, *What are my other students doing when I am working with small groups?* Choua, Stan, and Lena all reported that a major challenge for them in delivering effective reading instruction was providing students motivating, challenging independent learning activities that met their varying needs while they worked with guided reading groups and their EIR group. Therefore, this section details some of the differentiated literacy activities Choua, Stan, and Lena organized for their students during independent work time. Also provided are other suggestions and resources (Figures 6–1 to 6–12). With these ideas, you hopefully will feel more prepared to provide extra support to students in small groups using EIR emergent literacy strategies, just as Choua, Stan, and Lena did.

See the DVD for full-size versions of all the forms in this chapter.

Independent Activities in Choua's Classroom

Independent activities in Choua's classroom include reading and rereading familiar stories independently, with a partner, or in a small group; writing and drawing in a journal; writing and drawing on open response sheets; sharing with a partner what they have read or written about; and doing word work with a partner. For example, students:

▶ Write one of the summary sentences from a whole-group book/lesson on animal babies and draw an animal baby.

▶ Reread the guided reading group book.

My New Words

Name: _____ Date: _____

Write sight words from your small-group story [start with the letter _____] [have the C-V-C pattern and the vowel _____] [have the C-V-C-e pattern and the vowel _____], [are from the word family –V-C]. Use one or two words in sentences that tell about the story.

Words

_____

_____

Sentences

_____

_____

_____

_____

Figure 6–1 My New Words

Reading Log

Name: _____

Book Title	Date	Use words, or words and pictures to tell about your book

Figure 6–2 Reading Log

Practicing and Rating My Reading Fluency

Name: _____

Date: _____

Title: _____

I read my story _____ times.

a. **My tracking:**   Good 😊   Okay 😐   Could Be Better 🙁

b. **My phrasing:**   Good 😊   Okay 😐   Could Be Better 🙁

c. **My expression:**   Good 😊   Okay 😐   Could Be Better 🙁

I want to work on   a,   b,   c   (circle one).

Write or draw below to tell about your book.

_____

_____

_____

Figure 6–3 Practicing and Rating My Reading Fluency

Word Map

Name: _____   Date: _____

Title: _____   Page: _____

Write, or write and add pictures.

It means:	My connection:

Juicy word:

Sentence:	An example:

Figure 6–4 Word Map

Cause-Effect Chart

Name: _____

Title: _____

Date: _____

Write, or write and add pictures.

This happened (Cause)	That made this happen (Effect)	My ideas

Figure 6–5 *Cause-Effect Chart*

Topic Map

Name: _____

Date: _____

Write, or write and add pictures.

My animal is:	Where it lives:

What it eats:	Babies:

What it looks like:	Interesting facts:

Figure 6–6 *Topic Map*

Comparison Chart

[*Students should work on this in a small group with support from a skilled reader—a volunteer, educational assistant, older student helper.*]

Books: _____

Name: _____ Date: _____

	Animal 1: Wolf	Similar (S) or Different (D)	Animal 2: Coyote
Size, Looks Like	Big dog	D	Dog
Food	Animals:	S	Animals
Where It Lives	Woods	S	Lots of places
Interesting Facts	Pack	D	Alone

Figure 6–7 *Comparison Chart*

Narrative Summary Sheet

Name: _____

Book: _____

Write, or write and add pictures.

Beginning (who, where, problem):	Middle (events):

End (solution):	Author's message:

New Word

Write one new word and draw or write what it means.

Word	Page	Meaning

Figure 6–8 *Narrative Summary Sheet*

Summary Sheet for Informational Text

Name: _____   Date: _____

Write, or write and add pictures.

	Main Idea
PART 1	
PART 2	
PART 3	

New Word

Write one new word and what it means if you can.

Word	Page	Meaning

Figure 6–9   Summary Sheet for Informational Text

Writing About My Story

Name: _____

Date: _____

After listening to or reading a story, pick one or two prompts to write about in your journal. You can add pictures if you want.

▷ **My favorite part is** _____ **because** _____.

▷ **This story made me feel** _____ **because** _____.

▷ **I would like to ask the author** _____.

▷ **The author's message was** _____.

▷ **This book reminds me of** _____.

▷ **Write and draw your favorite part in the story. Tell why it was your favorite part.**

▷ **Compare two characters in the story. How were they alike? Different?**

▷ **Draw and label the main characters and tell about their part in the story.**

▷ **Make a connection. What did the story remind you of?**

Figure 6–10   Writing About My Story

Writing About My Informational Book

Name: _____

Date: _____

After listening to or reading a story, pick one or two prompts to write about in your journal. You can add pictures if you want.

▷ **Three interesting facts were . . .**

▷ **I learned . . .**

▷ **I wonder why or how . . .**

▷ **I want to learn more about . . .**

▷ **A connection I made was . . .**

Figure 6–11   Writing About My Informational Book

Book Sharing

Name: _____

Date: _____

After listening to or reading a story, pick one or two prompts to write about in your journal. You can add pictures if you want.

A. **Who is your book about?**

B. **Tell what happened in the story.**

C. **What was the problem? How did it get solved?**

D. **Do you like the book? Why or why not?**

E. **What is your favorite part of the story? Why?**

F. **This book reminds me of** _____.

Figure 6–12   Book Sharing

- Complete a response sheet based on small-group word work.

- Write and draw about the guided reading group book.

- Read from book bins.

- Complete a reading log and word map.

- Share their independent reading with a partner.

- Review letter names and sounds in an alphabet book with a partner and trace or write upper- and lowercase letters.

In the spring, Choua also has students prepare a research report with a partner on a topic of their choosing or a topic related to their social studies or science curriculum.

Independent Activities in Stan's Classroom

Stan creates independent activities (in which students work with partners and alone) that meet the varying needs of all the students in his class. Examples include:

- Draw a picture of something you remember about the story *Are You There, Baby Bear?*, share this with a partner, and reread the group sentence with partner.

- Complete a vocabulary web sheet for a read-aloud book.

- Write words and draw pictures to summarize the beginning, middle, and end of *The Little Red Hen*.

- Reread a guided reading group book and write and draw about it on a response sheet.

- Complete word work related to a guided reading group phonics lesson.

- Read a book from book boxes and respond in your journal.

- Read basic words on the word wall with a partner.

Stan constantly assesses whether the activities are challenging his students to become more skilled emergent readers, watching students closely as they participate in them, and reading and reviewing their work.

Independent Activities in Lena's Classroom

Lena's students usually can choose from among three or four activities. She often uses informational texts to excite and motivate her kindergartners. She has them find information in a number of books on the same topic and share what they have learned. Her students also write and talk about what they have read. For example, they might:

- Listen to a story on tape and then write and draw answers to questions, talk about the story with a partner, or complete a word web.

- Reread a small-group book.

- Make words with letter stamps and read the words with a partner.

- Write a summary of a whole-group book (with the help of the educational assistant).

More Suggestions for Challenging Independent Activities

Independent work time can be one of the most academically powerful junctures of the school day, because it's when students actually practice being the motivated, self-regulated learners we want them to be. The following additional activities sufficiently engage and challenge kindergarten students so they are less likely to go off-task into unproductive behavior. Making independent time work well is crucial because independence is the goal we're after—self-regulated, motivated learners.

What factors prevent kindergarten students from learning to read and learning to enjoy reading? Low-level tasks are one major factor. Research by Pressley and colleagues (2003) found that teaching behaviors that undermined academic motivation in primary grade classrooms included tasks with low-task difficulty in which students were asked to complete activities that were too easy, required low cognitive effort, and demanded little of them. Also students in these classrooms were given activities that were uninspiring, boring, simplistic, and lacked excitement or provided stimulation to students.

In my many visits to kindergarten classrooms over the 10 years I worked with schools on school-wide reading improvement (Taylor et al. 2005; Taylor 2011b), I often saw students engaged in primarily low-level tasks during independent work time. Typically, students in these classrooms were completing worksheets or workbook pages, coloring, cutting and pasting, and rereading stories more times than were warranted. Also, these activities often could be completed in much less time than the time allowed, which only compounded the likelihood that students dawdled, got off-task, chatted with students near them, or wandered around the room.

At the other end of the spectrum, on my school visits, I also went into classrooms in which students were participating in many tasks requiring high-level thinking and collaboration during independent work time. The levels of student engagement and the numbers of happy faces and excited eyes in these classrooms as compared to classrooms with less motivating activities were striking. Students typically had three or four activities to complete that kept them meaningfully engaged and working at a continuous, efficient pace. With enough to do and with interesting things to work on, they did not get off-task. Most importantly, they appeared to be happy learners.

These observations are supported by research of Pressley and colleagues (2003) on tasks that supported academic motivation in primary grade classrooms. They found that teachers had motivated learners when they engaged them in cooperative learning and high-order, critical, and creative thinking. For example, in kindergarten, students in groups of 3 or 4 might listen to a quality picture book on tape and respond to high-level questions that were written on a discussion card by the teacher, or two students might read about, collaboratively write, and co-present a research report on an animal of their own choosing. These teachers also used engaging and interesting texts that piqued students' curiosity, got them excited about their learning, and involved them in excellent literature.

Examples of independent work time activities to engage students and advance their literacy abilities are provided. Independent student response sheets that go with some of these suggestions are on the DVD-ROM (Figures 6.1–6.12).

For word sort sequences see *Words Their Way* (Bear et al. 2004).

For word family groupings, see *Words Their Way* by Bear, Invernizzi, Templeton, and Johnston (2004).

For more on Making Words, see *Phonics They Use: Words for Reading and Writing*, 5th ed. by Cunningham (2009).

For additional fluency suggestions, see *Fluency Strategies and Assessment* by Johns and Berglund (2005).

Activities That Support Word Recognition

▶ To reinforce students' knowledge of symbol–sound correspondence that you have recently taught in guided reading groups, have them complete word sorts with a partner. For example, if you have recently taught a group that there are two common sounds for *a*, short and long, you could have them sort words (or pictures that represent words) in the C-V-C and C-V-C-e pattern that contain short *a* or long *a*. A skilled reader (volunteer, educational assistant, older student helper) should check the words. To get practice reading words containing particular phonic elements, students should read the words that have been sorted.

▶ Have student partners write words that are part of a word family. A skilled reader (volunteer, educational assistant, older student helper) should check the words. Students should also read the words they have made (see Figure 6–1).

▶ Have students work with a partner or small group to generate words in a Making Words activity in which the directions have been written on a card by the teacher. To get practice reading words containing particular phonic elements, students should read words generated and sort words into word families.

Activities That Support Rereading

▶ Have partners reread stories from their guided reading group or EIR lesson, coaching one another on difficult words.

▶ Have students reread stories from their guided reading group or EIR lesson with a volunteer, educational assistant, or older student helper who can coach them if they get stuck on a word.

▶ Have students read new books for pleasure and list the books on a reading log (see Figure 6–2).

▶ Have students reread stories in their book box and rate their own fluency (see Figure 6–3).

Activities That Develop Vocabulary

▶ Have students write down and perhaps illustrate (on sticky notes or in a vocabulary journal) interesting, unknown, or newly learned words in the books they are reading. Students can share words and possible meanings with the teacher in whole- or small-group lessons, or with a volunteer, educational assistant, or older classroom helper.

▶ Have students complete a concept map or web (see Figure 6–4) of juicy words they find in the books they are reading.

For additional vocabulary suggestions see

Bringing Words to Life: Robust Vocabulary Instruction by Beck, McKeown, and Kucan (2002).

"Text Talk: Capturing the Benefit of Read-Aloud Experiences for Young Children" by Beck and McKeown (2001).

Activities That Support Comprehension: Skills and Strategies

Have students practice comprehension skills and strategies using open-ended response sheets: cause-effect sequence (Figure 6–5), topic map (Figure 6–6), comparison chart (Figure 6–7), narrative summary (Figure 6–8), informational text summary (Figure 6–9), writing about a narrative (Figure 6–10), writing about informational text (Figure 6–11).

For more suggestions for teaching comprehension skills and strategies, see

Reading and Writing Informational Text in the Primary Grades: Research-Based Practices by Duke and Bennett-Armistead (2003).

Informational Text in K–3 Classrooms: Helping Children Read and Write by Kletsien and Dreher (2005).

Activities That Support Comprehension: Learning New Information

Have students, if possible, with the support of a skilled reader (volunteer, educational assistant, older student helper):

▶ "Read" books to learn new information about topics of interest.

▶ "Read" books, magazines, and other texts related to the kindergarten social studies and science curriculum. Locate (with the help of the media specialist or volunteers) or purchase (with school funds, PTA funds, or donations from local businesses) books at various reading levels.

▶ Alone or with a partner or two prepare and give an oral talk (see Figure 6–12).

▶ Write down words to share (vocabulary) and write or draw pictures about the words from their independent reading (see Figure 6–4).

For more suggestions, see

Reading and Writing Informational Text in the Primary Grades by Duke and Bennett-Armistead (2003).

Informational Text in K–3 Classrooms: Helping Children Read and Write by Kletsien and Dreher (2005).

For more suggestions, see

Book Club: A Literacy Framework for Primary Grades by Raphael et al. (2002).

Using Literature to Enhance Content Area Instruction: A Guide for K–5 Teachers by Olness (2007).

For more suggestions, see

What Should I Read Aloud? by Anderson (2007).

Literature and the Child by Galda, Cullinan, and Sipe (2010).

Activities That Support Comprehension: Talk and Writing About Text

After you have modeled for and coached your students, have them:

- Listen to books on tape in the listening center.

- Respond to literature (see Figures 6–10 and 6–11).

- Prepare and give a book report (see Figure 6–12).

Activities That Support Reading for Pleasure

Have students:

- "Read" books from various genres for 10 or 20 minutes a day and complete a reading log (see Figure 6–2).

- "Read" different books from a favorite author.

- Share favorite books in a book club (see Figure 6–12).

- Write, rate, and draw pictures about favorite books on cards for a file that other students can look through for book suggestions.

Independent work time is an important component of teachers' overall classroom reading program. Students spend a considerable amount of time working on their own or with others while teachers work with small, guided reading groups. It is crucial that students are actively engaged in interesting, challenging learning activities that meet their needs and move them forward in literacy abilities during this independent work time. However, it is easy for these independent learning activities to become routine, undifferentiated, unnecessary practice, and not motivating or challenging to students. When this happens, it is easy for students to get off-task or spend much more time than is needed on assigned activities. To alleviate these issues, many teachers find that changing the independent activities every so often works well, as does providing students with choice. Additionally, providing students with long-term projects (e.g., author studies) can also avert some of the routinization of the activities. Furthermore, never underestimate the power of sharing ideas with colleagues about effective independent learning activities.

For more on effective, motivating reading instruction and assessment in general, see *Classroom Reading Assessment: Making Sense of What Students Know and Do* by Paratore and McCormack (2007).

Reading and Writing Grade by Grade by Resnick and Hampton (2009).

Reading Instruction That Works: The Case for Balanced Teaching by Pressley et al. (2003).

On Solid Ground: Strategies for Teaching Reading K–3 by Taberski (2000).

For more on differentiated reading instruction, see *How to Plan Differentiated Reading Instruction: Resources for Grades K–3* by Walpole and McKenna (2009).

Creating an EIR Community

E arly Intervention in Reading is a powerful approach for accelerating the
reading development of kindergartners who find learning to read difficult, and in some respects the EIR program is easy to implement. The
predictable structure, small-group attention, and motivating literature are
things teachers and children quickly grow to like. However, because the
approach includes a scope and sequence for teaching emergent literacy abilities
and a repertoire of teaching strategies, and because any learner who struggles
requires teachers to reflect and use considerable skill, I strongly encourage
teachers to enlist support along the following three lines:

1. Teachers need to work with colleagues during the first year of teaching EIR lessons.

As a classroom teacher, taking on EIR and weaving it into effective whole-group and small-group instruction requires highly differentiated teaching—not an easy thing to achieve. Also, teachers will not solve all of their students' reading problems unless they work collaboratively. A research study on effective reading practices (Taylor et al. 2000) found that the most effective schools had a collaborative model for delivering reading instruction in which struggling readers received a second, small-group reading intervention each day to accelerate their literacy learning.

Over many years, I have found that teachers experience more success with their students when they discuss EIR during monthly meetings with colleagues, who may include classroom teachers, Title I and other reading resource teachers, ELL teachers, and special education teachers. Together, teachers using EIR strategies for the first time can clarify procedures, share successes, and help one another solve problems.

2. Teachers need to get help with scheduling monthly meetings and one-on-one coaching conferences.

When a number of teachers are learning about and teaching EIR, having the support of a consultant or facilitator is extremely helpful. This person can secure EIR books and materials, schedule professional learning sessions, establish and monitor one-on-one word-recognition coaching by aides or volunteers, and solve problems as they arise.

3. Teachers need to do outreach with parents/caregivers, so that they can help their children practice reading at home.

Parents and guardians play a critical role. A sample letter explaining the program is provided in Figure 7–1 and on the DVD. You might also schedule an EIR information session at the beginning of the school year, perhaps as part of back-to-school night, in which you explain the materials you will be sending home and stress the importance of caregivers' involvement. (Have the children come along, serve cookies, and turn it into a festive event.) You might also invite caregivers to observe an EIR lesson in action in your classroom.

Overview of Monthly EIR Meetings

At monthly meetings of about an hour, teachers learning to teach EIR lessons gain expertise and confidence and hone their ability to develop children's emergent literacy skills and to pose questions about stories that lead to high-level, comprehension-building responses. By swapping successes, trials, classroom management ideas, and authentic independent activities teachers help one another become better teachers.

Begin the meetings in August or September and continue through May. If it's hard to find an hour once a month, meet for shorter times over several days during the month. For the first 10 or 15 minutes, focus on sharing ideas and concerns. Then spend 30 or 40 minutes reviewing and discussing EIR proce-

Figure 7–1 Parent Information Letter

Monthly Meetings Overview

August/September	Read and review Chapters 1, 2, 3, 4, and 6 Discuss instructional procedures and watch the DVD video clips related to Chapter 3 Review lessons and procedures for weeks 1–5 Review fall assessments Prepare for October meeting
October	Share your experiences teaching the week 1–5 lessons and review procedures as questions arise Review lessons and procedures for weeks 6–8 Review video-sharing procedures Prepare for November meeting
November	Share your experiences teaching the week 6–8 lessons and review procedures as questions arise Review video-sharing procedures Review lessons and procedures for weeks 9–11 Share videos of your teaching Prepare for December meeting
December	Share your experiences teaching the week 9–11 lessons and review procedures as questions arise Review lessons and procedures for weeks 12–15 Group Activity: Coaching for comprehension and book sharing Share videos of your teaching Prepare for January meeting
January	Share your experiences teaching the week 12–15 lessons and review procedures as questions arise Review lessons and procedures for weeks 16–18 Discuss coaching for comprehension Share videos of your teaching Prepare for February meeting
February	Share your experiences teaching the week 16–18 lessons and review procedures as questions arise Review and discuss lessons and procedures for weeks 19–21 Share videos of your teaching Prepare for March meeting
March	Share your experiences teaching the week 19–21 lessons and review procedures as questions arise Review lessons and procedures for weeks 22–24 Share videos of your teaching Prepare for April meeting
April	Share your experiences teaching the week 22–24 lessons and review procedures as questions arise Review lessons and procedures for weeks 25–27 Review spring assessment procedures Prepare for May meeting
May (if time permits, or at a grade-level meeting)	Share your experiences teaching the week 25–27 lessons and review procedures as questions arise Discuss results of assessments Review the year's results and discuss plans for next year

Table 7–1 Monthly Meetings Overview

dures and the video clips of effective practice provided on the DVD. By November, begin bringing in video clips capturing your own teaching of EIR lessons.

An overview of the yearly framework of professional learning sessions is provided in Table 7–1. Detailed suggested agendas for a year of monthly meetings begin on page 121. They include aspects of EIR to focus on, a structure for sharing and discussing progress and concerns, and protocols for viewing and sharing videos. Read through these agendas to get an idea of what a year of EIR professional development might look like, then use them to organize and promote your EIR work and learning.

August

In August, read and discuss Chapters 1 and 2 with the kindergarten teachers in your school who are participating in the EIR professional learning sessions. You may also want to read and discuss Chapter 6, which includes details about fitting EIR into your daily literacy instruction and making sure your independent activities are challenging, motivating, and engaging so you can focus your attention on the students in your guided reading groups and EIR follow-up group.

September

Additionally, in August or early September, begin to review the EIR procedures in Chapters 3 and 4. During the September and October meetings, go through the week 1–5 lessons in detail.

October

Sometimes teachers worry about "doing the EIR procedures correctly" and put off getting started. Don't be overly concerned at first about doing things "just right"; you'll get better at using EIR strategies over time. It's important to begin EIR lessons before or as close to October 1 as possible. Most children who will benefit from EIR need the small-group follow-up intervention all year. Students should have the opportunity to be a part of these small-group intervention lessons before feelings of discouragement set in. During this and subsequent monthly meetings, you can revisit aspects of the EIR procedures as questions arise.

November–May

Beginning in November, share videos of your teaching. Take turns bringing in a 5-minute (give or take) video clip of your EIR teaching to share, discuss, and reflect on. (Video-sharing procedures are described in greater detail later in this chapter and summarized in Figure 7–2. A sign-up sheet is provided in Figure 7–3.) So often, professional development focuses on the proper use of new materials. Teachers are rarely given the opportunity to think about, discuss, and enhance their own teaching practices with the help of colleagues. When sharing these videos focus on:

▶ What the children are doing well or the strengths they demonstrate.

▶ What the teacher is doing well to develop reading skills and strategies and foster independence and success in the children.

▶ What else the teacher might have done to develop reading skills and strategies and foster independence and success in the children.

Through EIR ongoing professional learning sessions, you will improve your coaching abilities. As you focus on coaching and work at it collaboratively, you are reminded that coaching children to become independent is not easy. However, you also learn that coaching is something you can master, with the end result of having more children in your classrooms reading well by the end of the school year.

Agendas for Monthly Meetings

September Meeting (70–75 min.)

Review of Chapters 1 and 2 (10–15 min.)

First talk about any questions or issues you have related to Chapters 1 and 2. You may also wish to discuss Chapter 6, which discusses how to fit EIR into your daily schedule and provide productive independent work for other students while you are working with your EIR group.

Discussion of Instructional Procedures in Chapters 3 and 4 (35–40 min.)

Carefully work through the EIR routines in Chapter 3 and watch the related video clips on the DVD. Then discuss the week 1–5 lessons in Chapter 4.

Review of Fall Assessments (20 min.)

Review the fall assessment procedures described in Chapter 5.

Preparation for October Meeting (5 min.)

Briefly review what needs to be done before the October meeting:

▶ Identify children who need EIR follow-up lessons. Don't worry if you aren't sure in some cases. You can ask questions in October and make changes then.

▶ Begin presenting EIR lessons as close to October 1 as possible and certainly before you meet again in October. You will get much more out of the October meeting if you have already started to teach EIR lessons. Jot down notes on this instruction so you can share your experiences and to get answers to your questions at the October meeting.

Often, teachers say they aren't ready to get started yet, but I tell them to simply "take the plunge" and realize that you will be getting better at teaching EIR lessons as the year moves along. The best way to learn about EIR instructional strategies is to start teaching EIR lessons. Good luck!

October Meeting (60–65 min.)

Status Report on EIR Teaching (15 min.)

▶ Based on the notes you have kept, discuss with other kindergarten teachers any problems and concerns that surfaced while teaching the week 1–5 lessons.

▶ As you discuss the week 4 and 5 lessons, focus on the skill of getting children to hear words in sentences. Many children don't understand the concept of a word within a sentence, and they need to do so before they can understand tracking and the alphabetic principle. Being able to count the number of words in a sentence helps them understand the concept of a word within a sentence. This is also an opportunity to model tracking print.

▶ Review and discuss Video 8.

Review of Video-Sharing Procedures (20 min.)

Each participant should share one video in November, December, or January and a second in February, March, or April. Share one or two videos each month; each segment should take no more than 15 minutes. (If you have more than six teachers in your group, break into two groups for the video sharing part of the meeting. Video-sharing groups of five or more should watch two videos a month; a three- or four-member group could watch only one, but two would of course be better if participants are willing to tape additional lesson segments.) To learn about video sharing, see Figure 7–2.

The basic approach to video sharing was developed for the EIR Professional Development Program but has also been used successfully in other teacher

---

Engaging in Video Sharing

The basic approach to video sharing was developed for the EIR Professional Development Program but has also been used effectively in other teacher professional development venues. Each video-sharing segment should take no more than 15 minutes. Focus on students' strategy use, independence, and success.

Prior to coming to your study group, do the following:

1. Videotape the lesson segment you selected. It should be about 5 minutes long.

2. Answer the following three video-sharing questions based on your video:

▶ What are the children able to do? What is going well?

▶ What are you doing to help children grow and be successful?

▶ What else could you have done to help children develop and be successful?

Share the video at a monthly meeting:

1. Present a minute of background about the lesson.

2. Call the group's attention to something you would like their help with.

3. View the video with the group.

4. Break into groups of three to review the three video-sharing questions. Take notes on things the children did well, things the teacher did well to help children develop and experience success, and suggestions for things you might have been done differently.

5. As a whole group, discuss the video-sharing questions (viewing the video again if necessary).

6. Collect the notes taken by the three-member groups and ask for your colleagues' ideas related to the aspect of your teaching you wanted help with.

Remember, this is first and foremost a learning activity in which colleagues are helping one another improve their skills in developing all students' emergent reading abilities. At an EIR session, sign up for a topic—one part of one day's lesson.

Video Sharing—Sign-Up Sheet for Kindergarten

Month	Teacher	Description of Video
November		Identifying rhyming words
		Acting out text
		Hearing number of words in a sentence
December		Phonemic awareness activities
		Review of letter names and sounds
		Story discussion, vocabulary, coaching for comprehension
January		Phonemic awareness activity
		Story discussion, vocabulary, coaching for comprehension
February		Interactive sentence writing
		Phonemic awareness activities
March		Sound boxes
		Interactive sentence writing
		Story discussion, vocabulary, coaching for comprehension
April		Tracking
		Sound boxes
		Word family work

Figure 7–2 Engaging in Video Sharing

Figure 7–3 Video Sharing—Sign-Up Sheet for Kindergarten

professional development venues (Taylor 2011b). Each video-sharing segment should take no more than 15 minutes. Focus on students' strategy use, independence, and success.

Prior to coming to your monthly meeting, do the following:

1. Videotape the lesson segment you selected (it should be about 5 minutes long).

2. Answer the following three video-sharing questions based on your video:

   ▶ What are the children able to do? What is going well?

   ▶ What are you doing to help children grow and be successful?

   ▶ What else could you have done to help children develop and be successful?

When you share the video at an EIR session, do the following:

1. Present a minute of background about the lesson.

2. Call the group's attention to something you would like their help with.

3. View the video with the group.

4. Break into groups of three to review the three video-sharing questions. Take notes on things the children did well, things the teacher did well to help children develop and experience success, and suggestions for things that might have been done differently.

5. As a whole group, discuss the video-sharing questions (viewing the video again if necessary).

6. Collect the notes taken by the three-member groups and ask for your colleagues' ideas related to the aspect of your teaching you wanted help with.

Remember, this is first and foremost a learning activity in which colleagues are helping one another improve their skills in developing all students' emergent reading abilities.

At an EIR session, sign up for a topic—one part of one day's lesson (see Figure 7–3 for the sign up sheet).

People should sign up for the video sharing in October (see Figure 7–3). If you have more than six teachers in your group, break into groups of three to five members for the video sharing part of the meeting. With six members in a video-sharing group, you would watch two videos a month. With three members in a video-sharing group, you would watch one video a month. Everyone should share their first video in November, December, or January, and a second video in February, March, or April.

Discussion of Grade-Level Procedures (20–25 min.)

▶ Review the week 6–8 lessons for November, focusing on the purpose and procedures for helping children hear the beginning sound in words. You may want to watch Video 3 (segmenting the beginning sounds in words from a story) and Video 6 (identifying pictures of things that begin with the sounds for *b* and *c*) again.

▶ Think about what books you will use for the different parts of each weekly lesson. You may want to review the sections in Chapters 3 and 4 on grade-level routines.

Preparation for November Meeting (5 min.)

For the November meeting, one or two people per small group should bring in short video clips showing them teaching a predetermined EIR skill, strategy, or activity. Teachers should sign up (see Figure 7–3) now for the videos they will present in November, December, and January.

November Meeting (60–75 min.)

Status Report on EIR Teaching (15 min.)

Share successes you experienced and questions that arose while teaching the week 6–8 lessons. If there are parts of the EIR routine you want to review, return to the relevant sections of Chapter 3 and the corresponding video clips or the example lessons in Chapter 4.

Review of Video Sharing Procedures (5 min.)

Discuss your questions, concerns, and feelings about sharing videos of your teaching.

Discussion of Grade-Level Procedures (20 min.)

Walk through the week 9–11 lessons for December. Discuss activities and help one another answer questions. Focus on students hearing the beginning and ending sounds in words. You may want to watch Video 4 again. Think about what books you will use for the different parts of the weekly lessons.

> ▶ Many teachers have children put their hand on their opposite shoulder when they say the beginning sound and move it to their wrist for the end sound. (Later they stop at the elbow on the middle sound.)
>
> ▶ Have children give the sounds in the words they are segmenting, not just the letter names. This helps them develop phonemic awareness.
>
> ▶ As you are segmenting sounds, try not to put an *uh* on the end of the consonants. For example, try to say /b/ /ee/ not /buh/ /ee/ for *be*. I discuss this issue in Chapter 3 and when presenting the directions for administering the phonemic awareness test in Chapter 5.

By now you are probably feeling more comfortable with the EIR lessons and routines. However, in November it is important to consider your timing in EIR lessons. You want to be sure you are getting to all of the parts of a lesson. Discuss strategies for getting through all parts of a lesson. If there are parts of the EIR routine that you want to review, return to the relevant sections of Chapter 3 and the corresponding video clips or the exemplar lessons in Chapter 4.

Topics to discuss in November include the following:

▶ The purpose of the alphabet book activities is to help children learn the letter names and sounds, but you need to move through this activity quickly as a review and leave sufficient time for the other lesson activities as well. Sometimes teachers spend more time on this than is necessary for a quick review. Talk about this issue.

▶ Share ideas on how you are fitting in the EIR target group and what the other children should be doing while you are working with the EIR target group.

Video Sharing (15–30 min.)

Share one or two videos, depending on the size of your group. Many teachers are nervous about doing this (a natural reaction), but it gets easier after you do it once. By May, most teachers feel that sharing the videos is one of the most valuable parts of their professional learning. So hang in there with the video sharing experience!

Preparation for December Meeting (5 min.)

Review who will be bringing in a short video clip of a particular segment of an EIR lesson. (See sign-up sheet.)

December Meeting (65–80 min.)

Status Report on EIR Teaching (10 min.)

Share successes you experienced and questions that arose while teaching the week 9–11 lessons.

Discussion of Grade-Level Procedures (15 min.)

▶ Walk through the week 12–15 lessons for January. Focus on the purpose of segmenting the sounds in three-phoneme words—to help children develop an aspect of phonemic awareness related to decoding unfamiliar words.

▶ *Small-group activity*: Briefly role-play segmenting three-phoneme words from *Do Like Kyla*. Focus on voicing consonants without putting an *uh* sound at the end of consonants.

Review of Coaching for Comprehension (10 min.)

By now you should feel comfortable teaching EIR lessons. It's time to turn your attention to coaching for comprehension. Keep a list of the questions you ask your students and jot down notes on your questioning practices to share at the January meeting. The following questions should get you thinking:

▶ Are you asking follow-up questions to prompt children to clarify what they are saying or elaborate on their ideas?

▶ Are you giving children enough wait time?

▶ Are you encouraging children who answer "I don't know" to talk instead of just moving on to another child?

▶ Are you asking questions that are based on a concept in the story but that leave the story behind and instead relate to children's lives?

▶ Are your questions thought provoking and meaningful?

Group Activity: Book Share (10 min.)

With a partner, examine books you will be using in future EIR lessons and generate some good coaching-for-comprehension questions. Share these with the larger group.

Video Sharing (15–30 min.)

Preparation for January Meeting (5 min.)

Review who will be bringing in a short video clip of a segment of an EIR lesson. Also remember to bring in notes on your coaching-for-comprehension experiences.

tip

▶ Many teachers have children put their hand on their opposite shoulder while saying the beginning sound, then move it to their elbow on the middle sound and their wrist on the end sound.

▶ Have children give the sounds in the words they are segmenting, not just the letter names. This helps them develop phonemic awareness.

▶ As you are segmenting sounds, try not to put an *uh* on the end of the consonants.

January Meeting (60–75 min.)

Status Report on EIR Teaching (10 min.)

Briefly report on successes you are seeing with your students—even after the holiday break! Discuss your experiences teaching the week 12–15 lessons.

Discussion of Coaching for Comprehension (10 min.)

At the December meeting, you were given these questions to help you focus on your questioning and coaching for comprehension:

▶ Are you asking follow-up questions to prompt children to clarify what they are saying or elaborate on their ideas?

▶ Are you giving children enough wait time?

▶ Are you encouraging children who answer "I don't know" to talk instead of just moving on to another child?

▶ Are you asking questions that are based on a concept in the story but that leave the story behind and instead relate to children's lives?

▶ Are your questions thought provoking and meaningful?

Discuss your notes and anything you learned about your practice.

Discussion of Grade-Level Procedures (20 min.)

▶ Walk through the week 16–18 lessons for February, in which you give the sounds for two- and three-phoneme words from a story, but not the words themselves (for example, "a big, black /k/ /a/ /t/ jumped out"), and ask children to blend the sounds together and come up with the words. During week 18 you pull some words from the story out of context and ask the children to put the sounds together, thereby taking away the clues provided by context. For example, after reading, ask, " What word is this from the story? /c/ /a/ /t/" from *Good Morning, Chick*. You may want to view Video 5 in which a kindergarten teacher blends sounds from a Mercer Mayer Little Critter story and asks her students to come up with words.

▶ Also focus on procedures for interactive sentence writing.

▶ *Small-group activity*: Briefly role-play blending three-phoneme words in context and in isolation using words from *Good Morning, Chick* (or your own book selected for this lesson).

Video Sharing (15–30 min.)

Also fill out a new video-sharing sheet (Figure 7–3) for February, March, and April.

Preparation for February Meeting (5 min.)

Review who will be bringing in a short video clip of a segment of an EIR lesson.

CATCHING READERS, GRADE K

February Meeting (60–75 min.)

Status Report on Children's Progress (10 min.)

I often say to EIR teachers that I love February because by this time I typically see that they are very excited about where their struggling readers are in reading. I hope this is true for you, but if not, don't be discouraged. Your students are making progress! Very briefly report on successes you are seeing with your students. Discuss any questions or reflections you have about teaching Lessons 16–18.

Discussion of Grade-Level Procedures (20 min.)

Walk through week 19–21 lessons for March. Focus on using words from a story just read aloud and helping children write the sounds of these words in boxes (one sound per box). Stick primarily to three-phoneme words with a short vowel sound but also include two- or three-phoneme words with a long vowel sound, such as *me* or *she*.

Group Activity: Writing Sentences (10 min.)

Discuss your challenges and successes with interactive sentence writing. If you have already had your children write sentences on their own, share your experiences.

Video Sharing (15–30 min.)

Preparation for March Meeting (5 min.)

Review who will be bringing in a short video clip of a segment of an EIR lesson.

March Meeting (60–75 min.)

Status Report on Children's Progress (10 min.)

Briefly report on successes you are seeing with your students. Share questions and reflections related to teaching the week 18–21 lessons.

Discussion of Grade-Level Procedures (30 min.)

Review the week 22–24 lessons for April. Beginning in week 22 you will focus on tracking print while reading story summaries. Accomplished kindergarten teachers help their students track while reading print (Taylor and Pearson 2000). Remember, your goal is exposure, not mastery.

In a national study of kindergarten instruction provided in effective schools and by accomplished teachers (Taylor and Pearson 2000), I found that the most accomplished teachers were more frequently observed helping their students track and read (as we do in lessons 22–24) than the least accomplished teachers. The teachers in the most effective schools were more frequently observed helping their children write for sounds (as we do with the sound box activity) than in the least effective schools.

Video Sharing (15–30 min.)

Engage in video sharing.

Preparation for April Meeting (5 min.)

Before the next meeting, read through the section in Chapter 5 on spring assessments. At the April meeting, you should review spring assessment procedures and answer any questions members of the group may have.

April Meeting (70–85 min.)

Status Report on Children's Progress (10 min.)

Briefly report on successes you are experiencing with your students. Share ideas and concerns related to the week 22–24 lessons. Discuss your successes, problems, and questions related to teaching children to track and decode words. Discuss plans for working with struggling readers next year.

Discussion of Grade-Level Procedures (15 min.)

Walk through the week 25–27 lessons for May. Focus on having students write C-V-C words from the same family.

Review of Spring Assessment Procedures (25 min.)

Review the steps for completing the assessments in Chapter 5. Select the passages you will all use from an informal reading inventory. (You should perform the assessments during the first two weeks of May before things get really wild at the end of the school year.)

Video Sharing (15–30 min.)

Engage in video sharing.

Preparation for May Meeting (5 min.)

Remind one another that you will be discussing your assessments, overall reflections about the year, and plans for next year.

May Meeting (60 min.)

Status Report on Children's Progress (20 min.)

Share any questions or reflections related to teaching the week 25–27 lessons. Share your major successes and challenges teaching EIR lessons this year.

Discussion of Assessment Results (20 min.)

Discuss how students did on the assessments and which assessments provided the most information. Were there any surprises? Did some students who you thought would do well not do well? Did some students do much better than you expected? How many students no longer need EIR? How many will require basic EIR next year?

Review of Year and Discussion of Plans for Next Year (20 min.)

Summary

I cannot overstress the importance of follow-up learning for students who need more literacy support and ongoing professional learning experiences for you as you present EIR instruction. These pieces of the program are key to its successful implementation, even though many think of them as "extras." The small-group follow-up lessons may be difficult to schedule, but it is imperative for struggling readers to receive as many opportunities as possible to practice and master reading. And teachers who participate in professional learning experiences with their colleagues feel much more confident about using the program.

I hope this book and the others in the Catching Readers series (for grades 1, 2, 3, and 4–5) will help you and your school meet your struggling readers' needs. Should you have additional questions, go to www.earlyintervention inreading.com, where you'll find additional resources and links for obtaining either in-person or telephone support from a colleague of mine trained in EIR. This intervention model is worth the time it takes. When you understand and implement EIR in your classroom, you will feel tremendous pride in what your students accomplish, knowing you were instrumental in showing them the way. I would like to close by saying "Thank You! Thank you for the important work you do for children and best wishes to you in your teaching!"

Works Cited

Adams, M. J. 1990. *Beginning to Read: Thinking and Learning About Print.* Cambridge, MA: MIT Press.

Anderson, N. A. 2007. *What Should I Read Aloud?* Newark, DE: International Reading Association.

Au, K. H. 2006. *Multicultural Issues and Literacy Achievement.* Mahwah, NJ: Lawrence Erlbaum.

Baumann, J. F., and E. J. Kame'enui. 2004. *Vocabulary Instruction: Research to Practice.* New York: Guilford.

Bear, D. R., M. Invernizzi, S. Templeton, and F. Johnston. 2007. *Words Their Way: Word Study for Phonics, Vocabulary, and Spelling Instruction.* 4th ed. Upper Saddle River, NJ: Pearson/Merrill Prentice Hall.

Beck, I. L. 2006. *Making Sense of Phonics: The Hows and Whys.* New York: Guilford.

Beck, I. L., and M. G. McKeown. 2001. "Text Talk: Capturing the Benefit of Read-Aloud Experience for Young Children." *The Reading Teacher* 55(1): 10–20.

Beck, I. L., M. G. McKeown, and L. Kucan. 2002. *Bringing Words to Life: Robust Vocabulary Instruction.* New York: Guilford.

Blachowicz, C., and P. Fisher. 2000. "Vocabulary Instruction." In *Handbook of Reading Research, Volume III*, ed. M. L. Kamil, P. B. Mosenthal, P. D. Pearson, and R. Barr. Mahwah, NJ: Lawrence Erlbaum.

———. 2002. *Teaching Vocabulary in All Classrooms.* 2d ed. Upper Saddle River, NJ: Pearson/Merrill Prentice Hall.

Bohn, C. M., A. D. Roehrig, and M. Pressley. 2004. "The First Days of School in the Classrooms of Two More Effective and Four Less Effective Primary-Grades Teachers." *The Elementary School Journal* 104: 271–87.

Chorzempa, B. F., and S. Graham. 2006. "Primary-Grade Teachers' Use of Within-Class Ability Grouping in Reading." *Journal of Educational Psychology* 98: 529–41.

Christensen, C. A., and J. A. Bowey. 2005. "The Efficacy of Orthographic Rime, Grapheme-Phoneme Correspondence, and Implicit Phonics Approaches to Teaching Decoding Skills." *Scientific Studies of Reading* 9: 327–49.

Clay, M. 1993. *Reading Recovery: A Guidebook for Teachers in Training.* Portsmouth, NH: Heinemann.

Common Core State Standards, www.corestandards.org/the-standards/english-language-arts-standards. 2010.

Connor, C. M., F. J. Morrison, and L. E. Katch. 2004. "Beyond the Reading Wars: Exploring the Effect of Child-Instruction Interactions on Growth in Early Reading." *Scientific Studies of Reading* 8: 305–36.

Consortium for Responsible School Change. 2005. *Description of Common Findings Across Multiple Studies on School Change in Reading.* University of Minnesota, Minnesota Center for Reading Research. www. cehd.umn/ reading/projects/school-change.html

Cunningham, P. M. 2009. *Phonics They Use: Words for Reading and Writing.* 5th ed. Boston: Pearson.

Cunningham, P. M., and D. R. Smith. 2008. *Beyond Retelling: Toward Higher Level Thinking and Big Ideas.* Newark, DE: International Reading Association.

Dolezal, S. E., L. M. Welsh, M. Pressley, and M. M. Vincent. 2003. "How Nine Third-Grade Teachers Motivate Student Academic Engagement." *Elementary School Journal* 103: 239–67.

Duke, N. K., and V. S. Bennett-Armistead. 2003. *Reading and Writing Informational Text in the Primary Grades: Research-Based Practices.* New York: Scholastic.

Edwards, P. A. 2004. *Children's Literacy Development: Making It Happen Through School, Family, and Community Involvement.* Boston: Pearson/Allyn & Bacon.

Foorman, B. R., and J. Torgesen. 2001. "Critical Elements of Classroom and Small-Group Instruction Promote Reading Success in All Children." *Learning Disabilities Research and Practice* 16: 203–12.

Foorman, B. R., C. Schatsneider, M. N. Eakin, J. M. Fletcher, L. C. Moats, and D. J. Francis. 2006. "The Impact of Instructional Practices in Grades 1 and 2 on Reading and Spelling Achievement in High Poverty Schools." *Contemporary Educational Psychology* 31: 1–29.

Fountas, I. C., and G. S. Pinnell. 1996. *Guided Reading: Good First Teaching for All Children.* Portsmouth, NH: Heinemann.

Fuchs, L. S., D. Fuchs, M. K. Hosp, and J. R. Jenkins. 2001. "Oral Reading Fluency as an Indicator of Reading Competence: A Theoretical, Empirical, and Historical Analysis." *Scientific Studies of Reading* 5: 239–56.

Galda, L., B. Cullinan, and L. Sipe. 2010. *Literature and the Child.* 7th ed. Belmont, CA: Thomson/Wadsworth.

Graves, M. F. 2007. "Conceptual and Empirical Bases for Providing Struggling Readers with Multifaceted and Long-Term Vocabulary Instruction." In *Effective Instruction for Struggling Readers K–6,* ed. B. M. Taylor and J. E. Ysseldyke, 55–83. New York: Teachers College Press.

Guthrie, J. T., A. Wigfield, and C. VonSecker. 2000. "Effects of Integrated Instruction on Motivation and Strategy Use in Reading." *Journal of Educational Psychology* 92: 331–41.

Guthrie, J. T., A. Wigfield, P. Barbosa, K. C. Perencevich, A. Taboada, M. H. Davis, et al. 2004. "Increasing Reading Comprehension and Engagement Through Concept-Oriented Reading Instruction." *Journal of Educational Psychology* 96: 403–23.

Hamre, B. K., and R. C. Pianta. 2005. "Can Instructional and Emotional Support in the First-Grade Classroom Make a Difference for Children at Risk of School Failure?" *Child Development* 76(5): 949–67.

Hasbrouck, J., and G. A. Tindal. 2006. "Oral Reading Fluency Norms: A Valuable Assessment Tool for Reading Teachers." *The Reading Teacher* 59 (7): 636–44.

Hiebert, E. H., and B. M. Taylor. 2000. "Beginning Reading Instruction: Research on Early Interventions." In *Handbook of Reading Research, Volume III*, ed. M. L. Kamil, P. B. Mosenthal, P. D. Pearson, and R. Barr. Mahwah, NJ: Lawrence Erlbaum.

Hiebert, E. H., J. M. Colt, S. L. Catto, and E. C. Gury. 1992. "Reading and Writing of First-Grade Students in a Restructured Chapter I Program." *American Educational Research Journal* 29: 545–72.

John, J. L., and R. L. Berglund. 2005. *Fluency Strategies and Assessments.* Dubuque, IA: Kendall-Hunt.

Juel, C., and C. Minden-Cupp. 2000. "Learning to Read Words: Linguistic Units and Instructional Strategies." *Reading Research Quarterly* 35: 458–92.

Kelley, M. J., and N. Clausen-Grace. 2007. *Comprehension Shouldn't Be Silent.* Newark, DE: International Reading Association.

Kletsien, S. B., and M. J. Dreher. 2005. *Informational Text in K–3 Classrooms: Helping Children Read and Write.* Newark, DE: International Reading Association.

Klingner, J. K., S. Vaughn, M. E. Arguelles, M. T. Hughes, and S. A. Leftwich. 2004. "Collaborative Strategic Reading: Real World Lessons from Classroom Teachers." *Remedial and Special Education* 25: 291–302.

Knapp, M. S. 1995. *Teaching for Meaning in High-Poverty Classrooms.* New York: Teachers College Press.

Kuhn, M. R., and S. A. Stahl. 2003. "Fluency: A Review of Developmental and Remedial Practices." *Journal of Educational Psychology* 95: 3–21.

Lapp, D., D. Fisher, and T. D. Wolsey. 2009. *Literacy Growth for Every Child: Differentiated Small-Group Instruction, K–6.* New York: Guilford.

Leslie, L., and J. Caldwell. 2006. *Qualitative Reading Inventory—4.* Boston: Pearson.

Lipson, M. L., J. H. Mosenthal, J. Mekkelsen, and B. Russ. 2004. "Building Knowledge and Fashioning Success One School at a Time." *The Reading Teacher* 57(6): 534–42.

Mathes, P. G., C. A. Denton, J. M. Fletcher, J. L. Anthony, D. J. Francis, and C. Schatschneider. 2005. "The Effects of Theoretically Different Instruction and Student Characteristics on the Skills of Struggling Readers." *Reading Research Quarterly* 40: 148–82.

McGee, L. M., and L. M. Morrow. 2005. *Teaching Literacy in Kindergarten.* New York: Guilford.

McKeown, M. G., I. L. Beck, and R. G. K. Blake. 2009. "Rethinking Reading Comprehension Instruction: A Comparison of Instruction for Strategies and Content Approaches." *Reading Research Quarterly* 44(3), 218–53.

National Reading Panel. 2000. *Teaching Children to Read: An Evidence-Based Assessment of the Scientific Research Literature on Reading and Its Implications for Reading Instruction.* Rockville, MD: National Institute for Child Health and Human Development, National Institutes of Health.

Oczkus, L. D. 2003. *Reciprocal Teaching at Work: Strategies for Improving Reading Comprehension.* Newark, DE: International Reading Association.

Olness, R. 2007. *Using Literature to Enhance Content Area Instruction: A Guide for K–5 Teachers.* Newark, DE: International Reading Association.

Paratore, J. R., and R. L. McCormack, eds. 2007. *Classroom Literacy Assessment: Making Sense of What Students Know and Do.* New York: Guilford.

Pikulski, J. 1994. "Preventing Reading Failure: A Review of Five Effective Programs." *The Reading Teacher* 48: 30–39.

Pinnell, G., M. Fried, and R. Estice. 1990. "Reading Recovery: Learning How to Make a Difference." *The Reading Teacher* 90: 160–83.

Pressley, M. 2001. *Effective Beginning Reading Instruction: Executive Summary and Paper Commissioned by the National Reading Conference.* Chicago, IL: National Reading Conference.

———. 2006. *Reading Instruction That Works: The Case for Balanced Teaching.* 3d ed. New York: Guilford.

Pressley, M., L. Mohan, L. M. Raphael, and L. Fingeret. 2007. "How Does Bennett Woods Elementary School Produce Such High Reading and Writing Achievement?" *Journal of Educational Psychology* 99 (2): 221–40.

Pressley, M., S. E. Dolezal, L. M. Raphael, L. Mohan, A. D. Roehrig, and K. Bogner. 2003. *Motivating Primary-Grade Students.* New York: Guilford.

Raphael, T. E., S. Florio-Ruane, M. Georg, N. L. Hasty, and K. Highfield. 2004. *Book Club: A Literacy Framework for Primary Grades.* Lawrence, MA: Small Planet.

Raphael, T. E., L. S. Pardo, and K. Highfield. 2002. *Book Club: A Literature-Based Curriculum.* 2d ed. Lawrence, MA: Small Planet.

Raphael, T. E., K. Highfield, and K. H. Au. 2006. *QAR Now.* New York: Scholastic.

Rasinski, T. V. 2003. *The Fluent Reader: Oral Reading Strategies for Building Word Recognition, Fluency, and Comprehension.* New York: Scholastic.

Resnick, L. B., and S. Hampton. 2009. *Reading and Writing Grade by Grade, Revised Edition.* Washington, DC: University of Pittsburgh and National Center on Education and the Economy.

Saunders, W. M., and C. Goldenberg. 1999. "Effects of Instructional Conversations and Literature Logs on Limited and Fluent English Proficient Students' Story Comprehension and Thematic Understanding." *The Elementary School Journal* 99: 279–301.

Snow, C. E., M. S. Burns, and P. Griffin, eds. 1998. *Preventing Reading Difficulties in Young Children.* Washington, DC: National Academy.

Stahl, S. A. 2001. "Teaching Phonics and Phonemic Awareness." In *Handbook of Early Literacy Research*, ed. S. B. Neuman and D. Dickenson, 333–47. New York: Guilford.

Taberski, S. 2000. *On Solid Ground: Strategies for Teaching Reading K–3.* Portsmouth, NH: Heinemann.

Taylor, B. M. 1991. A Test of Phonemic Awareness for Classroom Use. www.earlyinterventioninreading.com.

———. 1998. *A Brief Review of Research on the Learning to Read Process.* Minneapolis, MN: University of Minnesota.

———. 2001. *The Early Intervention in Reading Program: Research and Development Spanning Twelve Years.* www.earlyinterventioninreading.com.

———. 2010a. *Catching Readers, Grade 1.* Portsmouth, NH: Heinemann.

———. 2010b. *Catching Readers, Grade 2.* Portsmouth, NH: Heinemann.

———. 2010c. *Catching Readers, Grade 3.* Portsmouth, NH: Heinemann.

———. 2010d. "Predictors from Kindergarten and First Grade of End-of-First Grade Reading Achievement." Minneapolis, University of Minnesota.

———. 2011a. *Catching Readers, Grades 4/5.* Portsmouth, NH: Heinemann.

———. 2011b. *Catching Schools: An Action Guide to Schoolwide Reading Improvement.* Portsmouth, NH: Heinemann.

Taylor, B. M., B. Hanson, K. J. Justice-Swanson, and S. Watts. 1997. "Helping Struggling Readers: Linking Small Group Intervention with Cross-Age Tutoring." *The Reading Teacher* 51: 196–209.

Taylor, B. M., L. Harris, P. D. Pearson, and G. E. Garcia. 1995. *Reading Difficulties: Instruction and Assessment.* 2nd ed. New York: Random House.

Taylor, B. M., P. D. Pearson, K. Clark, and S. Walpole. 2000. "Effective Schools and Accomplished Teachers: Lessons About Primary Grade Reading Instruction in Low-Income Schools." *Elementary School Journal*, 101(2): 121–66.

Taylor, B. M., P. D. Pearson, D. S. Peterson, and M. C. Rodriguez. 2005. "The CIERA School Change Framework: An Evidence-Based Approach to Professional Development and School Reading Improvement." *Reading Research Quarterly* 40(1): 40–69.

———. 2003. "Reading Growth in High-Poverty Classrooms: The Influence of Teacher Practices That Encourage Cognitive Engagement in Literacy Learning." *Elementary School Journal* 104: 3–28.

Taylor, B. M., D. S. Peterson, M. Marx, and M. Chein. 2007. "Scaling Up a Reading Reform in High-Poverty Elementary Schools." In *Effective Instruction for Struggling Readers, K–6*, ed. B. M. Taylor and J. E. Ysseldyke. New York: Teachers College Press.

Taylor, B. M., D. S. Peterson, P. D. Pearson, and M. C. Rodriguez. 2002. "Looking Inside Classrooms: Reflecting on the 'How' as Well as the 'What' in Effective Reading Instruction." *The Reading Teacher* 56: 70–79.

Taylor, B. M., M. Pressley, and P. D. Pearson. 2002. "Research-Supported Characteristics of Teachers and Schools That Promote Reading Achievement." In *Teaching Reading: Effective Schools, Accomplished Teachers*, ed. B. M. Taylor and P. D. Pearson, 361–74. Mahwah, NJ: Lawrence Erlbaum.

Taylor, B. M., R. Short, B. Frye, and B. Shearer. 1992. "Classroom Teachers Prevent Reading Failure Among Low-Achieving First-Grade Students." *The Reading Teacher* 45: 592–97.

Valli, L., R. G. Croninger, and K. Walters. 2007. "Who (Else) Is the Teacher? Cautionary Notes on Teacher Accountability Systems." *American Journal of Education* 113: 635–62.

Van den Branden, K. 2000. "Does Negotiation of Meaning Promote Reading Comprehension? A Study of Multilingual Primary School Classes." *Reading Research Quarterly* 35: 426–43.

Walpole, S., and M. C. McKenna. 2009. *How to Plan Differentiated Reading Instruction: Resources for Grades K–3*. New York: Guilford.

Recommended Professional Readings

Resources on Phonemic Awareness

McCormick, C. E., R. N. Throneburg, and J. M. Smitley. 2002. *A Sound Start: Phonemic Awareness Lessons for Reading Success.* New York: Guilford.

Rog, L. J. 2001. *Early Literacy Instruction in Kindergarten.* Newark, DE: International Reading Association.

Resources on Phonics and Word Recognition Instruction

Bear, D. R., M. Invernizzi, S. Templeton, and F. Johnston. 2007. *Words Their Way: Word Study for Phonics, Vocabulary, and Spelling Instruction,* 4th ed. Upper Saddle River, NJ: Pearson/Merrill Prentice Hall.

Beck, I. 2006. *Making Sense of Phonics: The Hows and Whys.* New York: Guilford.

Cunningham, P. 2009. *Phonics They Use: Words for Reading and Writing,* 5th ed. Boston: Pearson.

Carnine, D. W., J. Silbert, E. J. Kame'enui, and S. G. Tarver. 2004. *Direct Instruction Reading,* 4th ed. Upper Saddle River, NJ: Pearson.

Taylor, B. M. 2010. *Catching Readers Grade 1.* Portsmouth, NH: Heinemann.

Resources on Fluency

Johns, J. L., and R. L. Berglund. 2005. *Fluency Strategies and Assessments.* Dubuque, IA: Kendall-Hunt.

Stahl, S. A., and M. R. Kuhn. 2002. "Making It Sound Like Language: Developing Fluency." *The Reading Teacher* 55(6): 582–84.

Resources on Vocabulary

Baumann, J. F., and E. J. Kame'enui, eds. 2004. *Vocabulary Instruction: Research to Practice.* New York: Guilford.

Beck, I. L., and M. G. McKeown. 2002. "Text Talk: Capturing the Benefit of Read-Aloud Experience for Young Children." *Reading Teacher* 55(1): 10–20.

Beck, I., M. McKeown, and L. Kucan. 2002. *Bringing Words to Life: Robust Vocabulary Instruction.* New York: Guilford.

Blachowicz, C., and P. Fisher. 2002. *Teaching Vocabulary in All Classrooms,* 2nd ed. Upper Saddle River, NJ: Pearson/Merrill Prentice Hall.

Resources on Comprehension Strategies

Duke, N. K., and V. S. Bennett-Armistead. 2003. *Reading and Writing Informational Text in the Primary Grades.* New York: Scholastic.

Kletsien, S. B., and M. J. Dreher. 2005. *Informational Text in K–3 Classrooms: Helping Children Read and Write.* Newark, DE: International Reading Association.

Raphael, T. E., K. Highfield, and K. H. Au. 2006. *QAR Now.* New York: Scholastic.

Resources on Comprehension: High-Level Talk and Writing About Text

Anderson, N. A. 2007. *What Should I Read Aloud?* Newark, DE: International Reading Association.

Beck, I. L., and M. G. McKeown. 2002. "Text Talk: Capturing the Benefit of Read-Aloud Experience for Young Children." *Reading Teacher* 55(1): 10–20.

Cunningham, P. M., and D. R. Smith. 2008. *Beyond Retelling: Toward Higher Level Thinking and Big Ideas.* Newark, DE: International Reading Association.

Galda, L., B. Cullinan, and L. Sipe. 2010. *Literature and the Child,* 7th ed. Belmont, CA: Thomson/Wadsworth.

Kelley, M. J., and N. Clausen-Grace. 2007. *Comprehension Shouldn't Be Silent.* Newark, DE: International Reading Association.

Olness, R. 2007. *Using Literature to Enhance Content Area Instruction: A Guide for K–5 Teachers.* Newark, DE: International Reading Association.

Raphael, T. E., S. Florio-Ruane, M. George, N. L. Hasty, and K. Highfield. 2004. *Book Club: A Literacy Framework for Primary Grades.* Lawrence, MA: Small Planet.

Wood, K. D., N. L. Roser, and M. Martinez. 2001. "Collaborative Literacy: Lessons Learned from Literature." *Reading Teacher* 55(2): 102–11.

Resources on Balanced, Differentiated Instruction

Fountas, I. C., and G. S. Pinnell. 1996. *Guided Reading: Good First Teaching for All Children.* Portsmouth, NH: Heinemann.

Lapp, D., D. Fisher, and T. D. Wolsey. 2009. *Literacy Growth for Every Child: Differentiated Small-Group Instruction, K–6.* New York: Guilford.

Manning, M., G. Morrison, and D. Camp. 2009. *Creating the Best Literacy Block Ever.* New York: Scholastic.

McGee, L. M., and L. M. Morrow 2005. *Teaching Literacy in Kindergarten.* New York: Guilford.

Morrow, L. M. 2003. *Organizing and Managing the Language Arts Block: A Professional Development Guide.* New York: Guilford.

Pressley, M. 2006. *Reading Instruction That Works: The Case for Balanced Teaching,* 3rd ed. New York: Guilford.

Routman, R. 2008. *Teaching Essentials.* Portsmouth, NH: Heinemann.

———. 2003. *Reading Essentials.* Portsmouth, NH: Heinemann.

Taberski, S. 2000. *On Solid Ground: Strategies for Teaching Reading K–3.* Portsmouth, NH: Heinemann.

Tyner, B. 2009. *Small-Group Reading Instruction: A Differentiated Teaching Model for Beginning and Struggling Readers.* Newark, DE: International Reading Association.

Walpole, S., and M. C. McKenna. 2009. *How to Plan Differentiated Reading Instruction: Resources for Grades K–3.* New York: Guilford.

Resources on Support for Struggling Readers

Fuchs, D., L. Fuchs, and S. Vaughn, eds. *Response to Intervention: An Overview for Educators.* Newark, DE: International Reading Association.

Taylor, B. M. 2010. *Catching Readers, Grade 1.* Portsmouth, NH: Heinemann.

———. 2010. *Catching Readers, Grade 2.* Portsmouth, NH: Heinemann.

Tyner, B. 2009. *Small-Group Reading Instruction: A Differentiated Teaching Model for Beginning and Struggling Readers.* Newark, DE: International Reading Association.

Vaughn, S., J. Wanzek, and J. M. Fletcher. 2007. Multiple Tiers of Intervention: A Framework for Prevention and Identification of Students with Reading/Learning Disabilities. In B. M. Taylor and J. E. Ysseldyke, eds., *Effective Instruction for Struggling Readers K–6* (pp. 173–95). New York: Teachers College Press.

Resources on Motivating, Effective Pedagogy

Connor, C. M., F. J. Morrison, and L. E. Katch. 2004. "Beyond the Reading Wars: Exploring the Effect of Child Instruction Interactions on Growth in Early Reading." *Scientific Studies of Reading* 8: 305–36.

Kelley, M. J., and N. Clausen-Grace. 2007. *Comprehension Shouldn't Be Silent.* Newark, DE: International Reading Association.

Manning, M., G. Morrison, and D. Camp. 2009. *Creating the Best Literacy Block Ever.* New York: Scholastic.

Olness, R. 2007. *Using Literature to Enhance Content Area Instruction: A Guide for K–5 Teachers.* Newark, DE: International Reading Association.

Pressley, M. 2006. *Reading Instruction That Works: The Case for Balanced Teaching,* 3rd ed. New York: Guilford.

Pressley, M., S. E. Dolezal, L. M. Raphael, L. Mohan, A. D. Roehrig, and K. Bogner. 2003. *Motivating Primary-Grade Students.* New York: Guilford.

Resources on Assessments

McKenna, M., and S. Stahl. 2003. *Assessment for Reading Instruction.* New York: Guilford.

Paratore, J. R., and R. L. McCormick, eds. 2007. *Classroom Reading Assessment: Making Sense of What Students Know and Do.* New York: Guilford.

Pressley, M. 2006. *Reading Instruction That Works: The Case for Balanced Teaching,* 3rd ed. New York: Guilford.

Taberski, S. 2000. *On Solid Ground: Strategies for Teaching Reading K–3.* Portsmouth, NH: Heinemann.

Resources on Culturally Responsive Instruction

Au, K. 2006. *Multicultural Issues and Literacy Achievement.* Mahwah, NJ: Lawrence Erlbaum.

Gaitan, C. D. 2006. *Building Culturally Responsive Classrooms: A Guide for K–6 Teachers.* Thousand Oaks, CA: Corwin.

For a list and review of books for teachers on English language learners, see Opitz, M. F., and J. L. Harding-DeKam. 2007. "Understanding and Teaching English-Language Learners." *The Reading Teacher* 60(6): 590–93.

Resources on Schoolwide Reading Programs and Effective Schools

Allington, R. L., and S. A. Walmsley, eds. 2007. *No Quick Fix: Rethinking Literacy Programs in American's Elementary Schools* (RTI ed.). New York: Teachers College Press.

Lipson, M. L., J. H. Mosenthal, J. Mekkelsen, and B. Russ. 2004. "Building Knowledge and Fashioning Success One School at a Time." *The Reading Teacher* 57(6): 534–42.

Morrow, L. M. 2003. *Organizing and Managing the Language Arts Block: A Professional Development Guide.* New York: Guilford.

Resnick, L. B., and S. Hampton. 2009. *Reading and Writing Grade by Grade, Revised Edition.* Washington, DC: University of Pittsburgh and National Center on Education and the Economy.

Taylor, B. M. 2011. *Catching Schools: An Action Guide to Schoolwide Reading Improvement.* Portsmouth, NH: Heinemann.

Taylor, B. M., and P. D. Pearson, eds. 2002. *Teaching Reading: Effective Schools/ Accomplished Teachers.* Mahwah, NJ: Lawrence Erlbaum.

Taylor, B. M., D. S. Peterson, M. Mar, and M. Chein. 2007. Scaling Up a Reading Framework for Prevention and Identification of Students with Reading/ Learning Disabilities. In B. M. Taylor and J. E. Ysseldyke, eds., *Effective Instruction for Struggling Readers K–6* (pp. 216–34). New York: Teachers College Press.